GCSE
AQA Business and
Communication Systems
The Revision Guide

This book is for anyone doing
AQA GCSE Business and Communication Systems.

Whatever subject you're doing it's the same old story — there are lots of
facts and you've just got to learn them. This one is no different.

Happily this CGP book gives you all that important
information as clearly and concisely as possible.

It's also got some daft bits in to try and make the whole
experience at least vaguely entertaining for you.

What CGP is all about

Our sole aim here at CGP is to produce the highest quality
books — carefully written, immaculately presented
and dangerously close to being funny.

Then we work our socks off to get them out to you
— at the cheapest possible prices.

Contents

SECTION SIX — THE INTERNET

SECTION SEVEN — WORD PROCESSING

SECTION EIGHT — SPREADSHEETS

SECTION NINE — DATABASES

SECTION TEN — OTHER SOFTWARE APPLICATIONS

> You'll see this symbol scattered throughout Sections 7 to 10.
> It means there's an animated tutorial to help walk you through an important
> practical skill. See the inside front cover of this book for more info.

ASSESSMENT TIPS

Published by CGP

Editors:
Helena Hayes
Andy Park
David Ryan
Michael Southorn
Katherine Reed

Contributors:
Colin Harber Stuart
David Morris
Ali Palin

With thanks to Victoria Skelton and Simon Little for the proofreading.

ISBN: 978 1 84762 409 3

Microsoft® and Windows® are either registered trademarks or trademarks
of Microsoft Corporation in the United States and/or other countries

Microsoft product screenshots reprinted with permission from Microsoft Corporation.

Groovy website: www.cgpbooks.co.uk
Jolly bits of clipart from CorelDRAW®
Printed by Elanders Ltd, Newcastle upon Tyne.

Based on the classic CGP style created by Richard Parsons.

Why Businesses Exist

Welcome to the Revision Guide for AQA <u>Business and Communications Systems</u> — this book could change your life. It probably won't be a major change, but it should help you to revise for your BCS exams. Let's start with some basics about <u>businesses</u>...

Most Businesses Have the Same Main Objective...

1) Businesses exist to provide <u>goods</u> or <u>services</u> to customers. Most businesses are <u>started</u> when somebody decides that they can <u>make goods</u> or <u>provide a service</u> that they can <u>sell</u> to people who are willing to <u>pay</u>.

2) It's a good idea for businesses to set themselves <u>objectives</u>. (An <u>objective</u> is anything that someone wants to <u>achieve</u> — for example, your objective in using this book is to get a better GCSE grade.)
For a <u>business</u>, one objective is more important than any other...

> 1) The <u>most important</u> objective (or <u>aim</u>) is to make a <u>profit</u> in order to <u>survive</u>. If a business does not make a profit it will go <u>bankrupt</u> and have to <u>close down</u>.
>
> Businesses will usually have other objectives too. For example...
>
> 2) Some will try to be the <u>biggest</u> in their <u>market</u>.
>
> 3) Others will try to provide the highest <u>quality</u> product possible.
>
> 4) Some might aim to maximise <u>sales</u> or <u>wealth creation</u>.
>
> 5) Others might be more concerned with <u>stability</u> — maintaining their <u>market share</u> or a <u>reasonable income</u>.
>
> 6) Other possible objectives include being <u>independent</u>, <u>satisfying customers</u>, or trying to limit the <u>environmental damage</u> caused.

D'oh... forgot to make a profit

Usually firms will only pursue these other objectives if it will <u>help make a profit</u> in the <u>longer term</u> — although firms with genuinely public-spirited owners might give up some profit for other objectives.

...But Some Businesses Have Different Priorities

1) For some businesses, profit is <u>not</u> their main objective.

2) This is either because it's a '<u>not-for-profit</u>' organisation (e.g. a <u>charity</u>) or it's in the <u>public sector</u> (which means it's owned by the <u>government</u> — like most schools and hospitals).

3) Not-for-profit organisations and public sector businesses need to earn enough income to <u>cover their costs</u>. Any <u>surplus</u> is then put back into the business.

4) Some profit-seeking businesses exist to achieve <u>social objectives</u> such as providing help for the homeless, or farmers in poorer countries. They're called <u>social enterprises</u> or '<u>more than profit</u>' organisations. This is because their <u>main aim</u> is to <u>use the profit</u> that they make for the <u>benefit of society</u>.

Different People Start Businesses for Different Reasons

Here are some possible reasons why people might want to start a business...

1) Lots of entrepreneurs (p2) have <u>financial objectives</u> — e.g. to earn a <u>huge fortune</u> or a <u>steady income</u>.

2) There might also be <u>non-financial</u> reasons, like the <u>freedom</u> of being your own boss.

3) For many people, running a business is a <u>challenge</u> that they enjoy.

4) Some people start a business because they want to <u>benefit others</u>. This could be done by starting a <u>charity</u>, or by having <u>social objectives</u> for their business.

I'd stick to the public sector — or you could end up in deep profit...

Well that's an easy enough page to start with. Make sure you know why businesses <u>exist</u> and why people <u>start them up</u>. You should also know what the <u>main objectives</u> of the different types of businesses are. <u>Cover</u> up the page, <u>scribble</u> it all down, and then <u>check</u> that you didn't forget anything. Champion.

Enterprise

Enterprise can mean either a business or organisation, or the personal qualities that mean you can see and take advantage of new business opportunities (e.g. "That boy will go far — he's got enterprise.")

Entrepreneurs Take Advantage of Business Opportunities

1) Enterprise involves identifying new business opportunities, and then taking advantage of them. There's always a risk of failure, but the reward for a successful enterprise activity is profit.

2) Enterprise can involve starting up a new business, or helping an existing one to expand by coming up with new ideas.

3) A good business idea is usually a product/service that no other business is already providing, but which customers will be willing to pay for — i.e. there's a gap in the market.

4) A market niche (or niche market) is a similar idea. A market niche is a small part of the overall market, and is made up of customers with a particular need. Big companies often don't bother trying to make products for niche markets, so they're great opportunities for small companies.

> An entrepreneur is someone who takes on the risks of enterprise activity.

Enterprise Means Taking Risks

Enterprises always involve balancing risks against possible rewards.

1) An entrepreneur needs to gather together all the resources needed to start or expand a business. The key resource is money, which is needed to buy equipment and pay workers.

2) Very often an entrepreneur will use their own money, but they'll probably need to raise more from banks or other investors as well.

3) An entrepreneur will hope that the business will make enough profit to pay back any money that's been borrowed. If not, the business will fail and the entrepreneur will lose all the money that's been invested in the company.

4) A good entrepreneur will take a calculated risk — they'll do research, plan the business carefully to make sure it has a good chance of success, and weigh up the consequences of failure. If the risk is worth taking, the entrepreneur will go ahead with the new business venture.

Entrepreneurs Need Particular Qualities

Well I'm looking in the bowl and I'm not seeing any of those round toffee ones. I need that particular quality Jones!

A successful entrepreneur is likely to have most of the following qualities:

- the ability to think ahead — to identify opportunities for the future
- initiative — to seek out or seize business opportunities
- drive and determination — to turn ideas into practice
- decisiveness — so they don't shy away from making tough decisions
- networking skills — to identify people who can provide money or other resources
- leadership skills and powers of persuasion — to motivate other people to support their ideas
- a willingness to take calculated risks — and to profit from their enterprise activities
- an ability to plan carefully — to minimise the risk of failure
- an ability to learn from mistakes — and to see mistakes as "part of learning to succeed"

Enterprise — think Dragons' Den... (or starships if that's more your thing)

Bit of a funny page this one, all about concepts and personal qualities. Don't worry though — you're about to dive headlong into some good old fashioned facts. For now though, I reckon you should make sure you know everything on this page. Yep, all of it. Even that bit right up there at the top.

Customers

There are lots of things that a business has to remember... and one of the most important things must always be its <u>customers</u>. Without customers, a business is nothing. <u>Nothing</u>, I say. And don't you forget it.

Finding Out What Customers Need is Essential

1) Without <u>customers</u>, a business can't <u>survive</u> — it's as simple as that.

2) So to succeed, a business has to make a product or provide a service that customers will be willing to <u>pay for</u>. There are a couple of different ways to approach this...

- <u>Market-driven</u> firms will find out <u>what people want</u>, then make it. This usually means the product is <u>useful</u> — like an MP3 player with a built-in radio.
- <u>Product-driven</u> firms will design or invent a <u>new product</u> and then <u>try to sell it</u>. This often means they make something <u>nobody</u> really wants — like an MP3 player with a built-in toaster.

3) With few exceptions, <u>market-driven</u> firms do <u>best</u>. This probably isn't all that surprising, since they start out with the customers' actual needs in mind.

A Business Should Never Forget its Customers

Worrying about customer needs or wants starts <u>way before</u> any product is actually made, and carries on <u>way after</u> they've bought something. (In theory, anyway.)

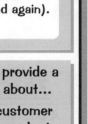
There's more about this on page 7.

Before customers make a purchase
- <u>Market research</u> is the process of <u>asking</u> customers what they want or need. It also involves finding out what products <u>competitors</u> provide, and at what price.
- Products must be designed and manufactured to be <u>reliable</u> and <u>fit for purpose</u> (i.e. to do the job they're supposed to) — customers don't want to have to keep phoning a helpline because their vacuum cleaner explodes every two weeks.

When customers make a purchase
Customer orders should be fulfilled accurately and on time. If a customer orders a ham and cheese pizza, don't send them a meat and potato pie. If you've <u>promised</u> next-day delivery, deliver the <u>next day</u> — don't turn up three weeks later saying you overslept.

There are two types of purchase:
- <u>Product trials</u> (when customers buy a product for the <u>first time</u> to <u>try it out</u>),
- <u>Repeat purchases</u> (when customers <u>come back</u> and buy the product again and again).

All businesses want customers to make repeat purchases.

After customers make a purchase
Many businesses have a customer service <u>department</u> — others train <u>all staff</u> to provide a good level of customer service. Some businesses do <u>both</u>. There's lots to think about...
- <u>After-sales support</u> and <u>warranties</u> — sometimes things go wrong, leading to customer questions and complaints — businesses need to put the problem right. Some products (e.g. cars and computers) might need to be serviced and updated throughout their life.
- Like the product itself, <u>customer service</u> needs to be <u>reliable</u> — e.g. you'd expect to have your call answered and the problem resolved <u>every time</u> you phone a <u>helpline</u>.
- Company <u>websites</u> can also provide customer services. Some companies let customers access services on the web (e.g. banks let their customers pay bills online). (There's more about how companies can use their websites on page 49.)

The tennis company failed — their service was broken...

Customer service is so important that companies often use <u>secret shoppers</u> to evaluate how they're doing. These are people who <u>pretend</u> to be customers, but who then <u>report back</u> on how they were treated. Sneaky.

Stakeholders

Everyone who is <u>affected</u> by a business is called a <u>stakeholder</u>, and different stakeholders often want different things from the business. There are two main types: <u>internal stakeholders</u> and <u>external stakeholders</u>.

Internal Stakeholders are Inside the Firm

I thought you said steakholder.

1) The most important stakeholders are the <u>owners</u>, who make a <u>profit</u> if the firm's successful, and can <u>decide</u> what the firm does.

- <u>Small</u> businesses are usually owned by the entrepreneurs who run the business.
- Larger businesses are often owned by <u>shareholders</u>. Shareholders don't usually work for the firm, but they will want the business to do well so that they receive a slice of the <u>profits</u>, and so that the <u>value</u> of their <u>shares</u> will increase.
- In some businesses, shareholders <u>delegate responsibility</u> for running the business (including deciding on its general direction, or <u>strategy</u>) to a <u>board of directors</u> (p10).

2) <u>Employees</u> (including <u>managers</u>) are stakeholders — they're interested in their <u>job security</u> and <u>promotion prospects</u>, as well as wanting <u>decent wages</u> and pleasant <u>working conditions</u>. Directors and employees may become <u>unemployed</u> if the company does badly.

External Stakeholders are Outside the Firm

A business has lots of external stakeholders — many of them wanting different things.

1) <u>Customers</u> are very important stakeholders — they want <u>high quality</u> products at <u>low prices</u>.

2) <u>Suppliers</u> are who the firm <u>buys raw materials</u> from, so the firm provides them with their income. They may face <u>cash-flow problems</u> if they do not get paid quickly enough, and will also <u>lose work</u> if the firm has to close.

I thought you said stay colder.

3) The <u>local community</u> where the business is based will suffer if the firm causes <u>noise and pollution</u> (which might also interest <u>environmental groups</u>). The local community may benefit if the firm provides <u>good jobs</u> and <u>sponsors</u> local activities. Firms may also provide <u>facilities</u> which the local community can use.

4) The <u>government</u> will receive <u>taxes</u> from the firm and its employees.

5) <u>Trade unions</u> will want good pay and working conditions for their members employed by the firm.

6) <u>Pressure groups</u> put pressure on firms to behave in particular ways. They might organise <u>demonstrations</u>, or <u>draw attention</u> to behaviour they don't approve of.

> Some people say that <u>competitors</u> are stakeholders too — since they're affected if they start to lose some of their customers to the firm.

The Most Important Stakeholders are the Shareholders

A business probably won't be able to satisfy <u>all</u> its stakeholders — it'll usually have to <u>compromise</u>.

1) No business can ignore its <u>customers</u>. If it can't sell its products it will go bust.

2) And if a business doesn't keep its workers happy it may become <u>unproductive</u>.

3) But a company may not mind being <u>unpopular</u> in the <u>local community</u> — if it sells most of its products somewhere else.

4) The one group no business can ignore for long is its <u>owners</u>/<u>shareholders</u>. Their interests lie at the heart of the business — if they're unhappy they can <u>sack</u> the directors or <u>sell</u> the business to someone else.

External Stakeholders
Local community
Customers   Government
Internal Stakeholders
Suppliers
Employees
Directors   Owners

Stakeholders — vampires are terrified of them...

Two key points... 1) there are <u>various</u> groups of stakeholders, and 2) <u>shareholders</u> usually get their way — after all, it's their business. A firm can't annoy its other stakeholders though — it's all about compromise.

Measuring Business Success

Examiners want you to tell them that there's <u>more</u> to being a successful business than just making a <u>big profit</u>. This page tells you about a few other ways to think about <u>success</u>.

A Firm and its Stakeholders may have Different Objectives

1) For a <u>business</u> to be successful it has to meet its <u>objectives</u> (see p1).
   The business will set itself <u>targets</u> to <u>measure</u> whether or not it has met its objectives.

2) The way that a business <u>coordinates</u> the activities of its various <u>departments</u> in order to try and achieve its objectives is called its <u>strategy</u> (this is decided by the directors — see p4).

3) But other stakeholders will have different opinions about what success is.
   Some of these might be in <u>conflict</u> with the objectives the <u>firm</u> sets itself.

Success for a Business Can Mean Different Things

Most stakeholders will define <u>success</u> using one or more of these ideas...

1) SURVIVAL is the main <u>short-term</u> objective of any business. Over two-thirds of new businesses close within five years of starting. Unless a business survives, it can't achieve its <u>other objectives</u>.

2) PROFITABILITY is important for many stakeholders, especially a business's owners.
   Profitable firms are an important source of <u>wealth creation</u> for the <u>economy</u>.

3) GROWTH can be measured in different ways — e.g. <u>number of employees</u>, <u>number of products sold</u>, or <u>income from sales</u>.

4) MARKET SHARE is found by <u>dividing</u> the <u>sales</u> of the <u>firm's products</u> into the <u>total sales</u> of the <u>market</u> (and multiplying by 100%). The <u>bigger</u> a firm's market share, the <u>greater</u> its ability to <u>control</u> the market.

5) CUSTOMER SATISFACTION measures how <u>happy</u> consumers are with the <u>products</u> and service provided by the firm. The firm can <u>measure</u> this by carrying out <u>customer opinion surveys</u>, a type of <u>market research</u>.

6) ETHICAL CONSIDERATIONS are about whether the company acts in a way that <u>society</u> believes is <u>morally right</u> (e.g. many consumers think that it's <u>wrong</u> to test cosmetics on animals).

7) ENVIRONMENTAL SUSTAINABILITY is about minimising the <u>impact</u> of the firm's activities on the <u>environment</u>.

You need to know how the <u>different stakeholders</u> will have <u>different ideas of success</u> based on their <u>interests</u>. Here are four examples — learn them.

I am an activist in a pressure group. I think most firms are too big and powerful. They pollute the environment and treat animals badly. I know they create lots of jobs but I think we'd be better off with a lower income and a healthier planet.

I'm a consumer. I want the firm to make good quality products at a low price — but I worry that some firms are too powerful and charge too much. I am also concerned about the environment but I can't always afford to buy environmentally friendly products.

I'm a shareholder. I want the firm to be as profitable as possible so I can earn a large dividend when the profit gets divided up. I don't care too much how the business achieves this, but I don't want the firm upsetting the other stakeholders too much — otherwise profitability might suffer.

I'm in the government. I want the business to create wealth and jobs for the economy — that way the voters will think I'm doing a good job and vote for me again at the next election.

Criteria — a place to have a coffee and shed a few tears...

The basic idea is that success can be <u>measured</u> — but different people will measure different things. Make a list of <u>objectives</u> that you think different stakeholders might have (see p4 for more about stakeholders). Then for each stakeholder find one or two objectives that might <u>conflict</u> with the interests of others.

Starting a New Business

Some of the biggest businesses you can think of started as just <u>one person</u> and a bloomin' good <u>idea</u>. But what makes an idea good, I hear you ask. Well... there are a few pointers on this page.

Successful New Businesses are Innovative not Inventive

<u>Invention</u> and <u>innovation</u> sound a bit similar, and mean similar things.
But there is a slight difference in meaning when you're talking about business.

1) If a new business is going to <u>succeed</u> it must <u>provide something</u> that other competitors do not.

2) An <u>invention</u> is a <u>new idea</u> — a new <u>product</u> or a new <u>method</u> of doing something, e.g. a new way to dry hair or make chocolate.

3) An <u>innovation</u> is a <u>successful introduction</u> of a <u>new idea</u>.

4) Creating a toaster that contains a radio would be an <u>invention</u>, but it would only be <u>innovative</u> if the idea was <u>successful</u> and people wanted to buy it.

Fudge teapots? No.
Pine-cone toothbrushes? No.
Think Tarquin, think!

Businesses Have to Add Value

<u>Adding value</u> means making a product that <u>customers</u> will pay <u>more for</u> than it cost the <u>business</u> to <u>produce</u>. It's all about making a product or service seem <u>more desirable</u> to a customer.
Here are <u>six</u> ways a business can add value to a product:

1) **USP** The secret is to have a <u>unique selling point</u> (USP) — something that makes your product <u>different</u> from your competitors' products. As long as customers <u>value</u> the USP they will <u>pay more</u> for your product.

This is the key to increasing sales — offering something that your competitors don't (or can't).

2) **DESIGN** Having a <u>good design</u> is important — e.g. clothes with <u>attractive</u>, <u>distinctive</u> designs are often more <u>desirable</u>. This means customers may be prepared to pay more for them.

These other ways of adding value are really just types of USP.

3) **QUALITY** People are often prepared to pay more for a <u>high quality</u> product. Some brands of car are <u>better built</u> than others, and the manufacturers <u>charge more</u> to reflect this.

It was when I heard branding was vital that I stopped wanting my own business. (Ouch.)

4) **BRANDING** Having a strong <u>brand image</u> is important. Some brands of portable MP3 player are more expensive than others, but people are happy to pay more because they have a <u>well-known</u> and <u>trusted</u> name. Brands that are seen as <u>fashionable</u> or '<u>cool</u>' also tend to be able to charge more for their products.

5) **CONVENIENCE** The product could be made more <u>convenient</u> — e.g. ready-grated cheese tends to cost more than blocks of cheese.

6) **SPEED** Customers may pay more to have a product <u>delivered quickly</u> — e.g. some firms <u>charge more</u> to deliver products the next day.

A commonly used benchmark of added value.

Try as I might, I can't find the USP for my digital camera...

Learn the <u>six</u> main ways successful businesses add value to their products. The trickiest bit here is the difference between <u>invention</u> and <u>innovation</u> — remember that innovation means bringing a new idea <u>successfully</u> to the market (you could remember that <u>mArket</u> and <u>innovAte</u> both contain the letter 'a').

Marketing and Market Research

Marketing is all the things a business does to separate people from their money — from designing a product people want, through to telling them where to buy it, and everything in between.

Learn the Four Ps of Marketing

But I can't see any Ps in marketing...

The four Ps are the key to understanding what marketing is all about.
If a firm gets them right it should be easy to sell its product.
If it gets even one of them wrong, it's in trouble.

THE FOUR PS OF MARKETING
Product
Price
Promotion
Place

Together the four Ps are called the MARKETING MIX.

1) The firm must come up with a product that people will want to buy. It must fulfil some of the customer's needs or wants.

2 The price must be one that the customer thinks is good value for money. This isn't the same as being cheap.

3) The product must be promoted so that potential customers are aware that it exists.

4) It must be sold in a place that the customer will find convenient.

1) Depending on the situation, some of the Ps might be more important than others. For example, if customers really want the product, they may be prepared to pay a higher price.

2) Customers' needs and wants usually change over time — a business should adapt its marketing mix to meet these changing needs.

Market Research Can Help a Firm Choose a Marketing Mix

There are two main types of market research (p3) a business can use:

1) PRIMARY RESEARCH is when a business does its own questionnaires and surveys.
   Primary research can be expensive and time-consuming, but contacting potential customers directly is the best way to find out about their preferences.

2) SECONDARY RESEARCH involves looking at data that's been published by other people.
   • It might include things like specialist market research reports, government publications, and articles in newspapers, magazines and on the internet.
   • Secondary research is cheap and instantly available. This can save time and money, but it may not be completely relevant to what the business wants to find out.

Data Can be Quantitative or Qualitative

The information that's found from market research is called data. Again, there are two basic types:

1) QUANTITATIVE DATA is anything you can measure or reduce to a number. If you're researching the pizza market, asking "How many chocolate pizzas will you buy each week?" will give a quantitative answer.

2) QUALITATIVE DATA can't be expressed in numbers. Market researchers often ask for feelings and opinions — e.g. asking "What do you think of chocolate pizzas?" will give a qualitative answer.

Qualitative data is tricky to analyse because it's hard to compare lots of people's opinions and draw strong conclusions. Good market research will use both types of information.

I want it all — and I want it now (in the right place at the right price, please)...
Customers are absolutely crucial to marketing. Market research can help firms to collect solid data about what their customers want. Interpreting this data can then help them to plan their marketing mix.

Analysing the Market

Businesses can't succeed without understanding <u>their</u> market — <u>market analysis</u> helps firms to find out who their <u>customers</u> are, what they <u>want</u>, and whether their needs are being met by the <u>competition</u>.

Businesses Map the Market to Find Market Gaps

A <u>market map</u> can help a new business to understand the <u>key features</u> of the market it's operating in. The kinds of information usually shown in a market map include...

1) The <u>number of customers</u> in the market — and how much they <u>spend</u>.
2) Which <u>market segments</u> the customers belong to.
   A market segment is a group of customers who all have something in common (e.g. they're in the same age group, the same location, or the same social class).
3) The products that are <u>popular</u> and <u>unpopular</u>.
4) <u>Competitors</u> selling similar products — and <u>where</u> they sell them.

1) Sometimes a market map will show up a group of customers with a need that <u>isn't being met</u>. This is called a <u>gap in the market</u>.
2) Businesses need to move quickly to fill the gap — <u>before</u> their competitors do. This usually means launching a new <u>product</u> or <u>service</u> that will meet the group's identified need.
3) A gap in the market can be a great <u>opportunity</u> for a business. If it gets the marketing mix right, a gap can <u>expand</u> to become a large market.

Businesses Need to Analyse Their Competitors

Businesses need to think about:

1) The strengths and weaknesses of competitors — most new businesses won't try to compete with the <u>strongest</u> aspects of other firms. It's usually much better to find an area where competitors are <u>weak</u>, and try to do those things <u>better</u> (e.g. if competitors are using out-of-date equipment, a new firm may be able to offer lower prices by using modern, more efficient equipment).
2) How their own products compare to others — the company might be able to <u>adapt</u> their product by looking at things that competitors do well.

Customer Preferences Don't Stay the Same Forever

Market research and market analysis can tell firms what customers want <u>at a particular time</u>. But customers' views and habits can <u>change</u> over time.

EXAMPLE

These pie charts show the results of Crazy Juice Ltd's <u>recent</u> research into <u>why</u> people buy their juice, as well as the results from similar research carried out in <u>1992</u>.

An analysis of the charts would include points like:
'Taste is still the most important factor,'
'Price is less important now than in 1992,'
or 'The biggest increase is in the fact that it's organic.'

Reasons for buying Crazy Juice — 1992
Advertising 10%, The fact that it's organic 5%, Taste 45%, Price 40%

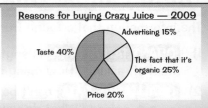
Reasons for buying Crazy Juice — 2009
Advertising 15%, The fact that it's organic 25%, Taste 40%, Price 20%

This analysis could lead to a new marketing mix based on the <u>quality</u> and <u>environmental friendliness</u> of the product.

I lost a molar — the tooth fairy saw a gap in the market...

All new firms need to <u>analyse</u> their market <u>before</u> they start doing business — if they don't, they run the risk of making a product customers <u>don't want</u>, or being flattened by <u>competing businesses</u>. Neither is cool.

Revision Summary for Section One

Okay, so that's the first section over with — now it's time to find out how much you remember. Have a bash at these questions. If you can do them all, pat yourself on the back and feel smug. If you can't, then go back and look at the section again and keep plugging away until you can answer them all. Yes, I know it's a pain but life's like that — and after all, it's the only way you're going to get ready for the exam.

1) What's the main objective for most businesses?
2) Describe objectives other than profit that a business might pursue.
3) Do charities aim to make a profit?
4) What is a social enterprise?
5) Give four reasons why people start their own businesses.
6) What is meant by a calculated risk?
7) List five qualities that an entrepreneur is likely to have.
8) Explain the difference between a market-driven business and a product-driven one. Which of these tends to be more successful?
9) What kind of information would market research aim to find out?
10) What kind of things can a business do to take care of customers once they've made a purchase?
11) Name six groups of stakeholders and say which are internal.
12) What role do the directors carry out in an organisation?
13) Who are the most important stakeholders and why?
14) List seven types of success that a company might hope to achieve.
15) Explain why the shareholders of a business and consumers might have different opinions about how successful the business is.
16) Explain the difference between an invention and an innovation.
17) Explain what is meant by a product having a unique selling point.
18) Describe six ways that a business can add value to their products.
19) What are the 4 Ps in the marketing mix? Explain what each one means.
20) Give an example of a situation where one marketing P might be more important than another. (If you're feeling enthusiastic, think up more than one example.)
21) Why do businesses usually have to change a product's marketing mix over time?
22) What's the difference between primary market research and secondary market research? Give one advantage and one disadvantage of each of these types of research.
23) Explain the difference between quantitative and qualitative data.
24) Explain what a market segment is, and give three examples.
25) Give three things (apart from market segments) that might be included on a market map.
26) What is a gap in the market? How can a new business take advantage of a gap?
27) Explain why it's important for businesses to analyse their competitors.

Organisational Structure

A large business could employ hundreds of people, all with <u>different skills</u> and levels of <u>experience</u>. The <u>structure</u> of the business describes how all the different people are organised.

Staff Work at *Different Levels* Within a Business

There are four basic <u>levels</u> of job that staff can have.

1) <u>DIRECTORS</u> are responsible for the business's <u>strategy</u> (its overall direction). The directors decide on strategy and targets at regular <u>board meetings</u>.

2) <u>MANAGERS</u> organise the carrying out of the directors' strategy. A large firm may have <u>senior</u>, <u>middle</u> and <u>junior</u> managers.

> Managers and supervisors are responsible for <u>planning</u>, <u>organising</u> and <u>decision-making</u> (see p12-13).

3) <u>SUPERVISORS</u> are ranked <u>below</u> managers. They usually look after <u>specific projects</u> or <u>small teams</u> of operatives.

4) <u>OPERATIVES</u> are workers who aren't responsible for other staff. They're often given <u>specific tasks</u> to perform by managers or supervisors.

Organisation Charts Show the Structure of a Business

A firm's structure can be shown on an <u>organisational chart</u>. Here are some examples...

1) A **HIERARCHICAL** firm is structured in <u>layers</u> — the directors are on the top layer, and operatives on the lowest layer. The number of people on each layer increases as you go down the hierarchy.

   In a firm with a 'tall' <u>hierarchy</u>, communication from the directors to the operatives can be <u>difficult</u> and <u>slow</u> because there are lots of layers to go through.

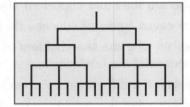

2) A **FLAT HIERARCHY** has <u>fewer layers</u> — this can make communication <u>clearer</u> and more <u>efficient</u>. But managers can get overwhelmed if they're in charge of too many people.

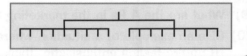

3) In a **MATRIX STRUCTURE**, groups of operatives work under <u>two or more</u> managers. In the diagram, the research operatives all work under the <u>research manager</u>. But each operative also works under one of the <u>project managers</u>, depending on which project they're involved in.

   A matrix structure is designed to encourage <u>flexibility</u> — allowing operatives to move easily to different projects (and project managers). But there may be <u>problems</u> if the two managers give the same operatives <u>conflicting tasks</u>.

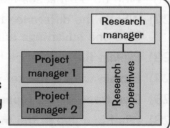

4) A **CIRCULAR CHART** arranges employees in circles. <u>Directors</u> and <u>senior managers</u> are at the <u>centre</u> of the circle, and <u>operatives</u> are on the <u>outside</u>. The idea behind circular charts is that no one's "at the bottom" (which can make people feel unimportant). They're supposed to be good for making people feel like part of a <u>team</u>.

To improve teamwork, draw a circular chart — simple...

Business structure is about <u>decision-making</u> and <u>communication</u>. Businesses can use these kinds of charts to spot potential <u>problems</u> with their structure — e.g. if a hierarchy has grown too tall over the years, then maybe decision-making will be too slow. These days, businesses use <u>ICT</u> to draw up this kind of chart.

Administration in Business

Businesses must have <u>quick access</u> to <u>accurate information</u>. This is why good <u>administration</u> is so important. It's not glamorous, but businesses <u>can't do without it</u>.

Administration Involves Four Main Activities

These are the four parts of "information administration" you need to know about. Learn them well...

1) `STORING` Information can be stored for future use using either <u>electronic</u> or <u>paper-based</u> filing systems.

2) `PROCESSING` Information can be <u>processed</u> to generate <u>new</u> information.
For example, <u>sales figures</u> can be processed to help decide future <u>production levels</u>.

3) `RETRIEVING` Stored information often needs to be <u>retrieved</u> and used again.
For example, last year's sales figures might be needed so they can be compared to this year's.

4) `DISSEMINATING` Information often needs to be <u>disseminated</u> (distributed) to other people and organisations. This could be done <u>verbally</u>, in <u>writing</u>, in <u>graphs</u> and <u>charts</u>...

ICT can make administration <u>faster</u>, more <u>accurate</u> and more <u>flexible</u> than paper-based filing — see Section 3 for more information.

Admin Helps All Parts of a Business to Operate Efficiently

1) Administration is vital for <u>all</u> the departments in a business — human resources, finance, operations, sales and marketing, customer service, research and development...

2) For example, human resources will need information about how staff are performing so that they can provide appropriate <u>support</u> and <u>training</u>.

See p14 for more about efficiency.

I'm not sure if this type of support is really appropriate, Liz.

Leah

3) Good administration helps businesses operate <u>efficiently</u>, and <u>compete</u> effectively.
- For example, having access to <u>up-to-date</u> and <u>reliable</u> information on <u>competitors</u> allows managers to make sensible, well-informed marketing decisions.
- <u>Administrative errors</u> can lead to <u>misleading</u> information being given to customers — e.g. a customer might be sent a bill for products they haven't ordered.
- If a company is <u>struggling</u>, it may need to <u>reduce its costs</u>. To do this effectively, it will need <u>accurate records</u> of how it <u>currently</u> spends its money before it can work out where to <u>reduce spending</u> in the future.

Good Admin is Vital for the Tax System

A business's <u>accountant</u> needs accurate information to look after a firm's finances.
For example, <u>financial records</u> are important when it comes to paying business <u>taxes</u>.

TAX

<u>Value Added Tax (VAT)</u> — depends on the difference between the price a business charges for its products and the amount they cost to make. So businesses need accurate records of what's been <u>paid to suppliers</u> and <u>received from customers</u>.

<u>Income Tax</u> and <u>National Insurance</u> — these depend on how much employees are paid, so a business needs accurate records of <u>how much</u> it <u>pays its workers</u>.

<u>Employers</u> have to deduct income tax and National Insurance from their <u>employees</u>' pay and give it to the government.

Employers also make an <u>extra</u> National Insurance payment for each person they employ.

<u>Corporation Tax</u> — depends on how much <u>profit</u> a business makes. Again, accurate <u>sales figures</u> and records of the firm's <u>total spending</u> are essential.

Processing your functions? Eww, too much information...

Business administration is all about handling <u>information</u>. <u>Accurate</u> administration is vital if a business is to run effectively. I reckon it's time to write a life-enhancing mini-essay all about admin and its importance.

Routine & Non-Routine Tasks

Business activities can be divided into <u>routine tasks</u> and <u>non-routine tasks</u> —
you need to know the difference between them and who might be involved in carrying them out.

Routine Tasks Can be Done by Operatives

1) In most businesses, there are certain tasks that need to be carried out <u>regularly</u>, and
   are basically the same each time. These are called <u>routine tasks</u>. Examples include:

   - <u>Storing documents</u> in the correct place so that they can be easily retrieved
     (either <u>paper</u> documents in filing cabinets, or <u>electronic</u> ones on computers).
   - Entering details of <u>invoices</u> into a <u>financial database</u> (or other data-inputting tasks).
   - <u>Re-stocking shelves</u> in a shop or supermarket.

2) Routine tasks can usually be done by <u>operatives</u> — they tend not to involve much <u>decision-making</u>.
   This doesn't mean they're not important — if routine tasks <u>weren't done</u>, the business would soon <u>suffer</u>.

3) The growth of ICT has meant that many routine tasks are now done by <u>computers</u> rather than humans.
   For example, <u>invoices</u> can be created <u>automatically</u> by a computer using stored information, and files can
   be automatically <u>backed-up</u> using basic software.

Non-Routine Tasks Often Involve Managers and Teams

1) Non-routine tasks are <u>less predictable</u> — they often involve high-level <u>decisions</u>. *See below for more about <u>decisions</u>.*

   - <u>Product development</u> — this requires <u>creativity</u> and technical expertise.
     Since a failed product could lead to huge losses, this needs the input of <u>experienced</u> staff.
   - <u>Recruiting new employees</u> — managers will need to look through all the applications and decide
     which candidates are the best. Decisions about recruitment are very <u>complicated</u> and are best
     made by <u>senior</u> members of staff, since employing the wrong person can be <u>expensive</u> for the
     company (and <u>unpleasant</u> for the employee).
   - <u>Upgrading equipment</u> — this involves <u>researching</u> and <u>comparing</u> the possible upgrade options.
     The firm then decides which will be best suited to its <u>present</u> and <u>future needs</u>, and its <u>budget</u>.

2) Non-routine tasks are often carried out by <u>teams of operatives</u>, with <u>managers</u>
   taking overall <u>responsibility</u> for the success or failure of the task.

3) Non-routine tasks can't usually be handled by computer software <u>alone</u>.

Decisions Can Also Be Routine or Non-Routine

Managers have more <u>responsibility</u> than operatives, and have to make tougher <u>decisions</u>.
Like tasks, decisions come in two flavours — <u>routine</u> and <u>non-routine</u>.

I hate routine decisions.

1) **ROUTINE DECISIONS** Routine decisions involve <u>day-to-day judgements</u>.
   These decisions are usually made by <u>operational managers</u> (the people in
   charge of teams of operatives) or by <u>operatives</u> themselves.

   Some routine decisions can be taken by <u>computers</u> — for example, a warehouse may use
   a software package to order more of an item when stocks drop below a particular level.

2) **NON-ROUTINE DECISIONS** These are more important decisions that may have a
   major effect on the business — deciding on the design of a new product, for example.
   As a result, non-routine decisions are generally made by <u>senior managers</u> or <u>directors</u>.

Routine-age kicks right through the night...

Don't be fooled by the name — routine tasks don't change much, but they're <u>crucial</u> for keeping businesses
running smoothly. Non-routine tasks involve more <u>decisions</u> — these are usually made by <u>managers</u>.

Planning

Anyone here like jazz? I love it. It's all crazy rhythms, squawking trumpet solos, and making it up as you go along. In business, everything's <u>planned out</u> in advance — it's not much like jazz. But I still love it.

Planning is About Making Decisions for the Future

1) <u>Planning</u> is vital in business. Planning means thinking about what the business is trying to <u>achieve</u>, and working out the <u>best way</u> to do it with the <u>resources available</u>.

2) Even for routine tasks, it's important to plan ahead — e.g. deciding <u>where</u> to store files. <u>Meetings</u> need to be planned carefully so that time isn't wasted on irrelevant discussions.

3) Planning can help to prepare for potential <u>problems</u> — for example, a firm might make a plan for dealing with a breakdown in its computer systems.

4) Planning also involves <u>prioritising</u> — deciding which activities are <u>most important</u>. <u>High priority</u> tasks will be dealt with <u>sooner</u>, and may be given <u>more resources</u>.

5) Access to <u>accurate information</u> is essential while making plans. For example, information about past projects, current projects, prices, competitors, changes in the market... etc. can all help while planning.

6) <u>Good</u> planning increases <u>efficiency</u>. <u>Bad</u> planning can mean projects are completed <u>late</u> or <u>over budget</u>. It can also <u>reduce quality</u> — e.g. if deadlines are <u>unrealistic</u> and staff feel pressured into <u>cutting corners</u>.

> I'll be using power point...

Planning Involves Several Stages

1 Identify your <u>objectives</u>

This means knowing:
- <u>what</u> it is you want to <u>achieve</u>
- <u>when</u> you need to achieve it by

2 Break the project down into <u>separate tasks</u>

Work out the <u>individual tasks</u> involved in completing the project. Prioritise the tasks — decide on the <u>order</u> these tasks will need to be performed in. Which ones need to be started <u>right now</u>? Can any be left until <u>later</u>?

3 Estimate the <u>time</u> needed for each task

- If you know how long the <u>individual tasks</u> in a project take, you can work out how long you'll need to complete the <u>whole project</u>.
- Decide whether you can do the separate tasks <u>one at a time</u>, or whether you'll need to do some of them <u>simultaneously</u>.
- Set <u>milestones</u> — these show <u>what tasks</u> need to be completed by <u>certain times</u> during the project. (Milestones help to keep projects <u>on schedule</u> — if a milestone is missed, then the project is running late and might not be completed in time.)

Using data from previous projects is often the best way to do this.

Compare the <u>total</u> project time to the <u>time limit</u> in your objectives.

You can then try to catch up — more people might be needed, or people may need to work overtime.

4 Identify the <u>resources</u> needed

This includes estimating: a) <u>materials</u>, b) <u>equipment</u>, c) <u>staff</u>, d) <u>money</u>.

> Ho, ho, ho — I'm ready to go!

> I think we've missed a milestone, Santa...

5 Think about how the project is affected by people <u>outside</u> the firm

For example, can suppliers provide <u>what</u> you need <u>when</u> you need it?

Listen carefully to this page — sounds like a plan...

Planning is about deciding on the <u>targets</u> that need to be met, and calculating the <u>time</u>, <u>money</u> and <u>other resources</u> that will be needed to meet them. Businesses aim for good plans based on sound <u>admin</u>.

Efficient Use of Resources

Businesses don't like <u>waste</u>. Wasted space, wasted time, wasted money... they all <u>reduce efficiency</u>. Also, <u>waste</u> has to <u>go somewhere</u> — and very often it ends up causing <u>pollution</u>.

Efficiency Means Getting Big Results from Few Resources

1) Efficiency is all about <u>achieving</u> your aims using as few <u>resources</u> as possible. ('Resources' means things like raw materials, money, staff, fuel... and so on.)

2) An <u>inefficient</u> business may achieve its aims, but <u>waste</u> a lot of resources along the way.

3) A firm that uses <u>few</u> resources but <u>fails</u> to <u>achieve</u> what it was trying to do is also inefficient.

Work Areas and Equipment Should be Efficient

The <u>buildings</u> and <u>equipment</u> a firm uses can have a big impact on its efficiency...

1) If a building is <u>too large</u> for the firm's needs, it may waste money on <u>rent</u>, <u>lighting</u> and <u>heating</u> (especially if the rooms are badly insulated). On the other hand, a <u>growing</u> business needs premises it can "<u>grow into</u>". Premises that are too <u>small</u> may mean the firm will soon need to <u>relocate</u> (which can be <u>expensive</u>).

2) The <u>design</u> and <u>layout</u> of buildings and work areas can affect efficiency too. Employees need <u>easy access</u> to equipment they use often (e.g. printers).

This abacus is an efficient investment — you can count on it.

3) But firms need to find a <u>balance</u>. For example, a firm could <u>save</u> its employees <u>time</u> if it bought them each a printer to put on their desk. But it'd need to be sure the time savings would be <u>worth</u> the expense.

4) Choosing <u>equipment</u> also involves a similar kind of <u>balance</u>. For instance, buying cheaper computers may <u>save money</u> in the <u>short term</u>. But if they can't cope with the needs of the business (e.g. if they're too slow), they'll be <u>inefficient</u>. This may cost the firm more in the long run.

Tasks Should Also be Designed Efficiently

1) Designing tasks efficiently means <u>planning</u> them so there's as little waste (of resources and people's time) as possible. See p13 for more information about planning.

2) Tasks should be done by staff with the right <u>skills</u>. This will mean <u>fewer errors</u> and <u>higher quality</u>. But getting <u>highly skilled</u> people to perform <u>fairly simple</u> tasks isn't the best idea — it'd be more efficient for them to be performing <u>more difficult</u> tasks.

3) And tasks should be timetabled so that staff don't <u>waste time</u> waiting for other tasks to be finished before they can start theirs.

The most <u>efficient</u> way to perform some <u>routine tasks</u> is to automate them using <u>ICT</u>.

Modern Businesses Need to Think About the Environment

1) <u>Energy efficiency</u> is important for the <u>environment</u>. Carbon emissions from fossil fuels like coal and gas are thought to contribute to <u>global warming</u> — firms are under pressure to <u>reduce</u> their use of these fuels.

2) <u>Resource depletion</u> is also a problem — the Earth's supplies of raw materials and fuels can't last forever. Firms need to use these resources efficiently, <u>reduce waste</u> and find <u>sustainable</u> alternatives for the future. Laws can help — e.g. there are regulations that encourage the <u>recycling</u> of electronic equipment.

3) But laws aren't always necessary. For example, lots of firms now <u>choose</u> to use <u>less packaging</u> for their products, <u>recycle</u> more, and use <u>recyclable materials</u> more often. These actions can help to <u>reduce costs</u>, and even <u>increase sales</u> — many customers prefer to buy from ethical, environmentally-friendly firms.

I sit in the car with the engine off and go nowhere...

... I'm on an efficiency drive. The basic <u>idea</u> of efficiency is pretty simple — in a nutshell it means <u>saving resources</u>. But very often you can <u>save</u> one resource (e.g. time) by using <u>more</u> of another (e.g. money). In practice, it's finding the right <u>balance</u> of resources to use that's tricky. But that's life, I suppose.

Office Layout

The layout of an office can affect how well staff do their jobs.
If the layout doesn't suit the type of work the business does, it can lead to <u>problems</u>.

There are Two Main Types of Office Layout

Open-Plan Offices

1) An open-plan office is one <u>large space</u> containing many desks.

2) Open-plan offices can <u>improve communication</u>, since staff sit together. They also make it <u>easier</u> to <u>supervise staff</u> (managers often work in the <u>same</u> office).

3) But open-plan offices can be <u>noisy</u>, which affects concentration. It also means there's little privacy — everyone might be able to hear you on the phone.

Cellular Offices

1) Cellular offices are <u>smaller rooms</u> with <u>solid walls</u>. These rooms are used by a <u>few workers</u> or just <u>one person</u>.

2) Cellular offices give staff <u>quiet</u> and <u>privacy</u> to do their work. They can often be <u>locked</u> to protect <u>valuables</u> or <u>confidential documents</u>.

3) A disadvantage of a cellular office layout is that it can make <u>supervision</u> of junior staff more <u>difficult</u>. It can also result in <u>less communication</u> between staff.

Hey! Who's sitting on my feet?

- The <u>nature of the tasks</u> staff carry out affects the layout of the office.
- For example, open-plan offices are often used in <u>call centres</u> (though these are sometimes divided up using temporary <u>partitions</u> into separate <u>cubicles</u>). This is efficient because lots of operators can be fitted into the space.
- But if employees need <u>privacy</u> for <u>confidential meetings</u> (e.g. between lawyers and their clients), then cellular offices are more suitable.
- These two basic layouts can be <u>combined</u>. For example, some offices have a large open-plan space surrounded by cellular rooms. This is useful if only a few employees (e.g. managers) need the privacy of a private office.

Ergonomic Design Makes Staff More Comfortable

Businesses need to <u>take care</u> of their employees. Partly because there are <u>laws</u> that say they have to (p17). But partly because it's <u>good business</u> — people who are permanently <u>uncomfortable</u> won't be very <u>efficient</u>.

Yeah, this new chair is great for my posture.

1) <u>Office equipment</u> (e.g. chairs, desks and keyboards) can be <u>ergonomically designed</u> — this means they're designed to be <u>comfortable</u>, and easy to use. For example, some office chairs can be <u>adjusted</u> to suit the needs of different users.

2) Poorly-designed equipment can lead to <u>back pain</u>, <u>eye strain</u> and <u>repetitive strain injury</u>. <u>Health and Safety laws</u> require businesses to minimise the risk of these injuries — using ergonomically-designed equipment can help them to do this.

Cellular office — a lock on the door and bars on the window...

If you want your staff to work effectively for 40 hours a week, they'll need to be <u>comfortable</u>. Managers also need to get the right balance between <u>supervising</u> staff and <u>trusting</u> them to work.

Modern Working Practices

Flexible working has become quite widespread in recent years. 'Flexible' means any pattern of work that doesn't follow the normal '35-hours-a-week in an office' kind of thing.

Flexitime Means Employees Can Vary Their Hours

I'm a flexible worker — geddit, boss?

No. Also, you're fired.

1) Employers are sometimes flexible about when employees work.

2) Some employers require their staff to work during core hours each week. But outside these core hours, they can work the rest of their weekly hours when they choose. This is known as flexitime working.

3) This can be good for employees as it gives them a greater sense of control over their working week.

4) But employers have to monitor work more closely to make sure that staff are still producing the required quantity and quality of work.

5) Part-time work (see p29) is also a form of flexible work pattern.

Work in Different Places — Teleworking and Hot-Desking

Employers are sometimes flexible about where their employees work (as well as when they work).

1) Teleworking is when people work away from their normal workplace — usually from home. Internet technology makes it possible for employees to transfer files and communicate easily from anywhere in the world. The advantage is that people don't have to travel into an office every day.

2) Hot-desking is when employees don't have their own special desks in an office. Instead, they sit at any free desk in an office — sometimes in a work centre used by more than one organisation.

3) Teleworking and hot-desking reduce the amount of office space needed by an employer, reducing costs. But it can make it harder to keep information secret, since data is regularly transferred away from a firm's own network into the 'outside world' (where it's harder to maintain security).

4) Teleworking means employees spend less time commuting and can fit their work more easily around home life. But it can be lonely, as there is less personal contact with colleagues. Hot-desking can also be stressful — never knowing where you're going to be working next.

Teleconferencing Links People in Different Places

1) Teleconferencing uses ICT to connect people in different locations using sound and/or video.

2) Locations are connected by a telecommunications system (e.g. a phone line, an internet connection, or a satellite link) so that several people can communicate. Examples of teleconferencing include:

- Audio conferencing — this is a bit like having a telephone conversation, only with more people. Everyone can hear what the others are saying, but they can't see each other.

- Video conferencing — this provides a video feed between the locations. Everyone can see and hear the others on monitors.

3) Teleconferencing saves time and money on travelling to a meeting place — people can hold meetings without leaving their offices.

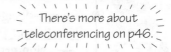
There's more about teleconferencing on p46.

Workin' flexitime — what a way to make a livin'...

A lot of office workers still work 9 till 5 every day, but modern ICT makes it possible to do things differently. Staff may enjoy having more flexibility, but it doesn't necessarily suit everyone. As usual, learn it all.

Health and Safety at Work

There are laws to help ensure people don't get <u>ill</u> or <u>injured</u> at work.
The laws make health and safety the <u>responsibility</u> of both the <u>employer</u> and <u>employees</u>.

Employers Need to Follow Health and Safety Legislation

The <u>Health and Safety at Work Act 1974</u> means <u>everyone</u> is responsible for health and safety.

<u>Businesses</u> have to:
- <u>assess</u> the risks involved in a job,
- take <u>precautions</u> to minimise these risks,
- provide <u>protective clothing</u> and <u>equipment</u>, and make sure it is <u>well maintained</u>,
- provide any <u>training</u> needed to do a job safely,
- provide <u>toilets</u>, <u>drinking water</u> and <u>first-aid</u> facilities,
- <u>record</u> workplace injuries in an <u>accident book</u>.

<u>Employees</u> have to:
- act <u>responsibly</u>, and take care of <u>their</u> and <u>other people's</u> safety
- carry out tasks as they've been <u>trained</u> to do
- <u>report</u> dangerous practices

This is to help <u>identify hazards</u> and prevent future accidents.

Computer Use can Cause Health Problems

Computers look pretty safe, but they can cause various health problems.

1) <u>Repetitive strain injury</u> (<u>RSI</u>) means aches, pains and muscle or tendon damage resulting from overuse of a keyboard or mouse. And <u>circulation</u>, <u>fitness</u> and <u>back</u> problems might result from sitting all day in front of a computer. These are <u>long-term</u> health problems.

2) Spending too long in front of a computer screen can cause <u>eye strain</u> and <u>headaches</u>. The Display Screen Equipment Regulations 1992 set out rules concerning the use of computers.

Employers must:
- <u>Analyse</u> workstations and <u>reduce risks</u>.
- Plan work routines so that employees can take <u>periodic breaks</u> from using a computer.
- Provide health and safety <u>training</u> and <u>information</u>.
- Provide <u>free eye-tests</u> to all staff who regularly use computers as part of their job.

IFY OUCA NREADTHI SYOURENOTW ORKINGHARDENOUGH

Employers and Employees Have Responsibilities

So how do these laws on computer use affect the typical office — well, let me explain...

1) Employers should allow employees to take regular <u>breaks</u> from computer work. Employees should use these breaks to <u>walk</u> around and <u>exercise</u> their fingers and hands.

2) Employers have a responsibility to provide <u>suitable equipment</u>, e.g. <u>desks</u>, <u>chairs</u>, <u>keyboards</u> and <u>screens</u>. (A 'suitable' screen, for example, would allow staff to adjust its <u>brightness</u> and <u>position</u>.)

3) Employers also have to provide training in how to use this equipment (e.g. how to arrange it properly, how to sit without straining your back). Employees then need to follow this training.

4) Employers and employees have to take precautions to reduce risks to everyone's safety. For example, they should make sure <u>electrical cables</u> aren't in places where people can trip over them.

Don't worry — reading this book won't give you eye strain...

Employers and employees need to be aware of health and safety. Draw a <u>table</u> with the <u>problems</u> ICT can cause in one column and the <u>solutions</u> in another column. Careful with that pen, though — it looks sharp.

Revision Summary for Section Two

That was the best. Section. Ever. Organisational structure, admin, planning, office layout... awesome. You don't look very convinced. Maybe young people don't say 'awesome' any more.

Still, some revision questions will probably be enough to change your mind. Try the ones below — if you get any wrong, read up on the bits you didn't remember and try again. The usual drill.

1) Explain the role of each of the following types of staff in a business.
    a) Directors   b) Managers   c) Supervisors   d) Operatives

2) Give one advantage that a flat hierarchy has over a tall hierarchy.
   Explain one possible disadvantage of a flat hierarchy.

3) Explain what a matrix structure is, and give one advantage and disadvantage of this structure.

4) Explain one advantage of using a circular chart to show a firm's structure.

5) Explain the four main activities involved in business administration.

6) How can good administration help businesses to be efficient?

7) What records would a business need in order to calculate each of these?
   a) Value Added Tax (VAT)   b) Income Tax   c) Corporation Tax

8) Give some examples of routine tasks in a business. Which type of staff usually does routine tasks?

9) Explain why non-routine tasks are usually performed by higher-ranking staff than routine tasks.

10) What's the difference between routine and non-routine decisions?
    Which type of staff are most likely to make each type of decision?

11) Give one reason why it's important to plan for a business meeting.

12) Explain three problems that can be caused by poor planning.

13) Describe five processes that may be involved in planning a business project.

14) What does it mean for a business to be efficient?

15) Explain how the size of business premises can affect a firm's efficiency.

16) Give two reasons why businesses are being encouraged to use fossil fuels more efficiently.

17) Give three ways that businesses can use materials more efficiently.
    Give two benefits that this can have for the business.

18) What's the difference between open-plan offices and cellular offices?
    Give one advantage and one disadvantage of each type.

19) What does it mean for office equipment to be ergonomically designed?

20) Why might a firm want to provide ergonomically-designed equipment to its staff?

21) Describe how flexitime works, and give one advantage that it has for employees.

22) Explain what teleworking and hot-desking are.

23) Give one advantage and one disadvantage of teleworking to: a) Employers   b) Employees

24) Give one advantage of teleconferencing.

25) Give three things that employers can do and three things that employees can do
    to reduce health and safety risks at work.

26) Explain three problems that can be caused by using computers for long periods of time.

27) Give a brief description of what employers must do according to
    the Display Screen Equipment Regulations 1992.

Data Processing Systems

Right... a page about <u>data-processing systems</u>. (Don't worry... it's not as bad as you might think.)

Businesses Need to Collect and Process <u>Data</u>

1) Business data can come from all sorts of <u>sources</u>.

2) <u>Primary data</u> is collected <u>first-hand</u> by the business itself.
<u>Secondary data</u> is information that's been collected by someone <u>outside</u> the firm.

3) But whatever the source, data needs to be <u>relevant</u> and <u>accurate</u>.

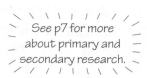

See p7 for more about primary and secondary research.

Data Systems Can be <u>Paper-Based</u> or <u>Computer-Based</u>

Data is <u>stored</u>, <u>processed</u> and <u>communicated</u> using a <u>data system</u>.
Two very important things to know about any data system are the <u>purpose</u> and the <u>medium</u>.

① PURPOSE   <u>What</u> a data system needs to <u>do</u>. You need to know this before you can <u>design</u> or <u>evaluate</u> a data system.

② MEDIUM   Data systems can be <u>paper-based</u> or <u>computer-based</u>.

Purpose... porpoise... medium... no... well, I tried.

You need to know the pros and cons of both <u>paper-based</u> and <u>computer-based</u> systems.

PAPER-BASED SYSTEMS
- These are useful when <u>hard copies</u> (i.e. paper versions) of documents are needed.
- These systems don't need computer equipment, and staff won't need computer <u>training</u>.
- But paper documents can take up a lot of <u>storage space</u>.
- And paper-based systems don't allow for easy <u>data processing</u> — it has to be done by hand.

COMPUTER-BASED SYSTEMS
- These require <u>less storage space</u> — a single PC can store as much data as many stacks of paper. And it's easy to create <u>backup copies</u> of electronic files.
- Data can be <u>processed</u> quickly and accurately. Files can also be viewed and changed on-screen, so it's easier to <u>edit</u> documents.
- Computers can be linked together in <u>networks</u>. This makes it easy to share data. But it can also means that confidential data needs to be very carefully <u>protected</u> (see p26).

Most of this section is about computer-based data systems. They're made up of <u>hardware</u> and <u>software</u>.

③ HARDWARE   <u>Hardware</u> means the bits of kit you can actually <u>touch</u> (e.g. keyboards, printers and so on).

Most of this section is all about hardware and software.

④ SOFTWARE   Software means the programs used on the computer — the <u>operating system</u> (e.g. Windows® or Linux) and <u>applications</u> (e.g. word processors, spreadsheets).

Like my dad said — you can't fight the (data) system...

A data-processing system means the <u>methods</u> and <u>equipment</u> businesses use to deal with information. <u>Computer-based</u> systems are now most common, but keeping <u>paper copies</u> is still important to most firms. A lot of the time the <u>purpose</u> of your data system will involve <u>communicating</u> information from one person or place to another — there's a lot more about communication in Section 5, so come back to this page and have another look once you've read that. Okay... now that I've said that, it's on with the show...

Computers and Input Devices

Here we go then... the first of quite a few pages all about <u>hardware</u>. First off, the <u>computer</u> itself.

Computers Can be Desktop or Portable

1) <u>Desktop</u> computers are relatively large and are designed to be used in a single place.

2) <u>Laptops</u> are smaller and <u>portable</u>. <u>Netbooks</u> are smaller still.

Shown to scale

3) <u>Handheld computers</u> include Personal Digital Assistants (PDAs), e.g. <u>Smartphones</u>. They often have a touch-sensitive screen or a small keyboard. Most PDAs also include a mobile phone and <u>internet</u> access.

A desktop computer and a mobile phone (circa mid-80s).

4) Computers can be connected together to form a <u>network</u>. This makes it possible for them to <u>communicate</u> with each other.

5) A network file server is a powerful computer that stores files users have made and 'runs' the network. Network <u>workstations</u> give users access to the network.

Shown to scale

The choice of computer will depend on...

1) <u>Where</u> the computer will be used: desktop PCs are perfect for an office. But if you're going to be moving around, you'll need something more portable.

2) The <u>tasks</u> that need to be done: desktops with large monitors are ideal if you're going to be creating detailed documents all day long. A smartphone wouldn't be so good for this.

3) The <u>cost</u>: technology is expensive — firms have to live within their means.

Keyboards are the Most Common Input Devices

An input device is any hardware that's used to enter data onto a computer — a keyboard, for example.

1) <u>QWERTY keyboards</u> are based on the way <u>typewriters</u> were designed. The name comes from the <u>first row of letters</u> on the keyboard.

2) Keying in can be <u>slow</u> unless the user has been trained to type, but QWERTY keyboards are so standard that most people can use them pretty well.

3) Long-term keyboard use can sometimes cause <u>repetitive strain injury (RSI)</u> (see p17).

Concept keyboards and touch-sensitive screens

<u>Concept keyboards</u> are most often found in <u>shops</u> and <u>restaurants</u>. Each key has a <u>symbol</u> (or word) on it, representing a piece of data stored in the computer (e.g. a <u>price</u>).

They're <u>great</u> if you want to key in similar data <u>over and over</u> again. But they're only designed for inputting very <u>limited</u> types of information.

<u>Touch-sensitive screens</u> are a bit like concept keyboards — but instead of pressing a key, you touch the picture or word on the screen. Again, they're easy to use. And you can have different options each time the screen display changes. But they're more <u>expensive</u> than a keyboard.

A Mouse is Used for Pointing and Clicking

1) Mice tell the computer the <u>direction</u> and <u>speed</u> they're being pushed in — this is used to control a pointer.

2) A mouse can make using a computer much quicker than a keyboard alone, but, again, using a mouse for long periods can cause <u>repetitive strain injury</u>.

Use the smart bomb.
Use the smart bomb.

Madam, please leave the operating theatre.

Joysticks also react to hand movements — they are mainly used to control devices such as <u>robots</u> or <u>hospital body scanners</u>. They are also sometimes used to play <u>games</u>.

Q: What do you call a broken mouse? A: Pointless.

Providing a specialised input device is one way that an employer might be able to <u>adapt</u> the workplace to allow a person with a disability to work more easily (see the <u>Equality Act</u> on p32). For example, a <u>head-wand</u> allows someone with limited mobility in their arms to use a keyboard.

More Input Devices

Can't get enough of input devices? Then you'll love this page. It's got data capture forms on it. Phwoar...

Digital Cameras and Scanners Convert Images into Data

1) Digital cameras capture real images and convert them into data which can then be uploaded onto a computer and edited.

2) Images can then be posted on the internet or sent as email attachments.

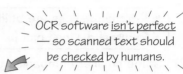
OCR software isn't perfect — so scanned text should be checked by humans.

3) Scanners are similar to digital cameras, except they digitally capture images of paper documents.

4) OCR (Optical Character Recognition) software can then turn scanned text into text that can be edited using word-processing software.

Ahahahahaaa! Ahaha! Ha.

Many retailers, especially supermarkets, use EPOS (Electronic Point of Sale) devices such as laser scanners. These scanners read product bar codes which the store's computer system uses to automatically add up prices and adjust stock records.

5) Webcams are basically digital cameras. But they're usually used to take pictures (and record video footage) for streaming (showing) over the internet.

Microphones are an Increasingly Common Input Device

Dear sir, Thank you for your letter dated 19th May...
Yeah!
Dear sir, Thank

1) Microphones are used to capture sounds, which can be stored digitally or streamed over the internet.

2) They can also be used with voice-recognition systems, which convert speech into text or into commands for the computer. This means you can use dictation instead of having to type (but the systems aren't always 100% reliable).

This is another way that employers can adapt the workplace to allow a person with certain disabilities to work more easily.

Data Capture Forms are Used to Collect Data

Data capture forms are also used for inputting data — but they're not hardware like the other input devices. They're paper forms, or computer software — data is written or typed onto them.

MANUAL DATA FORMS — the information is collected by hand, usually on paper.

- For example, a customer might write down information on an order form and post it to a business.
- The main drawback is that the information then needs to be entered into a computer by another person. This can lead to mistakes — e.g. by misreading the information on the form.

ELECTRONIC DATA FORMS enable users to enter information directly into the computer system.

- For example, a form on a website might enter data into a database (see page 68).
- The data is entered directly by the user (i.e. no one else has to read the form and type the data in) — this should mean fewer mistakes. Most systems also carry out validation checks — e.g. if there's information missing, you won't be able to move on to the next part.
- The main drawback is that the user needs to be connected to the computer system.

Input your left leg in, your left leg out — in, out, in, out...

...shake it all about. You do the Hokey-Cokey and you turn around... that's what it's all about.
Oh, hang on — that's not what it's all about. It's all about input devices. Sorry — off in a world of my own.
Right... an easy page, this. But make sure you actually know it — don't just skim over it and assume you could answer any questions about this stuff in an exam just because you've used a digital camera on holiday.

Data Storage

Businesses can have huge amounts of data that need to be <u>stored securely</u> and <u>accessed easily</u> — often by lots of people. Luckily, there are plenty of options to choose from when it comes to data storage.

Storage Devices Can be Internal or External

1) There are <u>two</u> main types of computer storage devices...

> • <u>Internal devices</u> are built into a computer (e.g. a hard disk).
> • <u>External devices</u> can be removed from a computer (e.g. a DVD or a USB stick).

2) Some smaller companies use their computer's hard drives (<u>internal</u> devices) as the <u>main</u> form of storage. This can work fine, but it's best to <u>back up</u> data regularly as well (see next page).

3) Larger firms tend to store information on a central <u>server</u> on their network so that all staff have access to it. This centrally held data can easily be <u>backed up</u> onto an <u>external</u> device.

4) <u>Portable</u> storage devices can be used for <u>backing up</u>, or transferring files between <u>different computers</u>.

Hard Disks are Usually Internal Storage Devices

1) Most computers have an internal <u>hard disk</u>.

2) Storage capacity of hard disks is usually measured in <u>gigabytes</u> (GB). One gigabyte is the same as 1024 <u>megabytes</u> (MB).

3) The storage capacity of hard disks gets larger all the time. But <u>desktop</u> computers generally have more storage space on their hard drives than <u>laptops</u> (it's to do with the lack of physical space inside a laptop).

Whadda you lookin at?

4) If a hard drive <u>fails</u> all the data on it can be <u>lost</u>. So it's sensible to keep <u>back-ups</u> of data files on an <u>external</u> storage device.

5) You can also get <u>external hard disks</u>. These <u>portable</u> devices plug into a computer to provide even more storage capacity — they're also useful for <u>backing up</u> hard drives.

Memory Cards and Memory Sticks Store Data on Chips

1) <u>Memory cards</u> and <u>memory sticks</u> can't hold as much data as hard disks. But they're small enough to be carried in a <u>pocket</u> or <u>purse</u>.

I'd never remember my recipe for toadstool broth without it.

> • <u>Memory cards</u> (e.g. SD cards or Compact-Flash cards) fit into small memory slots in digital cameras, smart phones or computers.
> • <u>USB sticks</u> fit into USB slots on a computer.

2) They allow you to easily <u>transfer</u> data between electronic devices, since they can be unplugged from one computer and plugged into another.

3) They can create <u>security problems</u> though. They're easily lost, for example. It's also easy to copy <u>confidential information</u> onto them or transfer <u>viruses</u> onto company networks. Some businesses <u>don't allow</u> their employees to use them.

Make sure memory sticks stick in your memory...

Memory sticks and hard disks are common ways of storing data, but they're <u>not perfect</u> for all purposes. Small memory sticks are easy to accidentally <u>lose</u>/flush down the toilet, and hard disks can be <u>corrupted</u>. Given this, there's nowt like <u>backing</u> up all your data... just in case. See the next page for more...

Data Storage and Back-Up

A second page about <u>data storage</u>, and some stuff about <u>backing up</u> — hold on to your hats...

CDs and DVDs Can Be _Read-Only_ or _Rewritable_

Compact Discs (CDs)

<u>CDs</u> hold about 700 MB of data. There are several different types:

1) **CD-ROM** — these are <u>read only</u> — the data held on them <u>can't be altered</u>. ◄ ⌐ROM = Read-Only Memory⌐

2) **CD-R** — you can write data to a <u>blank CD-R</u>.
But... once you've written the data, you <u>can't change</u> it. ◄ ⌐R = Recordable⌐

3) **CD-RW** — these have the advantage that data
on the disk can be <u>erased</u>, and the disk <u>reused</u>. ◄ ⌐RW = ReWritable⌐

Digital Versatile Discs (DVDs)

DVD — these are like CDs but hold <u>more data</u> — about 8 GB.
And like CDs...
- some DVDs are <u>read-only</u>,
- some can be written to <u>once</u>,
- some can be <u>written to</u> and <u>erased</u>.

Behold the magical Disc of Rainbows!

1) CDs and DVDs are great for storing <u>audio</u> and <u>video</u> to use at home,
but <u>aren't ideal</u> for most business data.

2) This is because it takes a relatively <u>long time</u> to write data onto them.
And there's no quick way to <u>edit</u> a file and <u>save</u> the changed version onto the disc.
It's also easy to <u>scratch</u> the discs, making them <u>unreadable</u>.

Magnetic Tape and Web-Based Storage

1) <u>Magnetic Tape</u> is <u>cheap</u> and it has a <u>huge storage capacity</u>.
Companies often use magnetic tape to <u>back up</u> their electronic data.
But accessing data on magnetic tape can be <u>slow</u>.

2) <u>Web-based file storage services</u> allow data to be <u>uploaded</u> to the internet, and
<u>downloaded</u> again when it's needed. This is an example of <u>remote storage</u> — the
data is stored in a completely separate place from the computer that writes the data.

Storage Devices Can be Used to Back Up Data

1) Any storage device can be <u>lost</u>, <u>stolen</u>, <u>damaged</u> or <u>destroyed</u>.
Data can also be <u>corrupted</u> (<u>accidentally</u> or by <u>viruses</u>) or <u>lost</u>.

2) For this reason, it's important for businesses to
<u>back-up</u> their data (i.e. make a <u>copy</u>).

⌐Backed-up files are often <u>compressed</u> (reduced in size) to <u>save space</u>.⌐

3) Backing up data can cost a business <u>time</u> and <u>money</u>, but losing all their data could be much <u>more costly</u>.
Making back-up copies of a company's data can take a <u>long time</u> — it's often done <u>overnight</u>.

4) Back-ups are usually stored in a <u>different location</u> (in case the firm's main building is <u>burgled</u> or damaged
by <u>fire</u>). Ideally the backed-up data should be stored in a <u>locked fireproof room</u>.

Plan A — always have a back-up plan...

Okay... another page about <u>storage devices</u>. There are all sorts of ways that a business can store its data.
But whatever storage devices it uses, it's <u>vital</u> to make sure that data is <u>backed up</u> and stored safely — that
way, any data that gets lost can be <u>retrieved</u>. Write down the pros and cons of all these storage methods.

Output Devices — Printers

An <u>output device</u> is any hardware used to <u>communicate</u> results of processing data.
Let's talk about printers....

Businesses Often Need Hard Copies

1) Printers produce <u>hard copies</u> of documents (a <u>hard copy</u> means it's printed out on paper).

2) Businesses often need to produce hard copies — sometimes to create a <u>permanent record</u>, but sometimes because it's the most appropriate way to <u>communicate</u> with <u>customers</u>.

3) But printing documents out on paper usually works out more <u>expensive</u> than looking at them <u>on screen</u>. (There's the cost of the <u>paper</u> and <u>ink</u>, as well as the cost of <u>maintaining</u> the printer.)

There are Different Kinds of Printer

Laser Printers are Fast and High Quality

Laser printers are the best choice for <u>larger</u> businesses that print <u>a lot</u> of documents.

Advantages of Laser Printers	Disadvantages of Laser Printers
• They can print <u>high-quality</u> documents.	• They can be <u>quite expensive</u>.
• They're <u>fast</u> — usually over 10 pages per minute (ppm).	• They contain a lot of <u>complex equipment</u> — so they're <u>expensive to repair</u>.
• Laser printers are <u>very quiet</u>.	• They can't use <u>continuous</u> or <u>multi-part</u> stationery.

Ink-Jet Printers are Cheap and Reasonable Quality

1) These <u>cost less</u> to buy than laser printers, but they're not quite as slick.

2) Small <u>jets of ink</u> are sprayed through tiny <u>nozzles</u> onto the paper.

> The <u>resolution</u> of a printer (the detail it can print) is usually measured in <u>dots per inch</u> (<u>dpi</u>)

3) Ink-jet printers are great for <u>small</u> businesses that don't produce a lot of paper — they provide <u>good quality</u> at a <u>reasonable price</u>.

4) For larger businesses, they're just <u>too slow</u>, and the quality isn't top-notch.

Advantages of Ink-Jet Printers	Disadvantages of Ink-Jet Printers
• <u>Good resolution</u> — although usually not as good as a laser printer.	• <u>Slow(ish)</u> — colour printing is often less than 4 pages per minute.
• Can be <u>cheaper to buy</u> than laser printers.	• <u>Quite expensive to run</u> — the ink costs more (per page) than laser cartridges.
• <u>Small</u> — so ideal for home or office desk use.	

Dot-Matrix Printers are Old-Fashioned and Slow

Dot-matrix printers use <u>pins</u> and an <u>inked ribbon</u> to create patterns of <u>dots</u> — these dots form <u>characters</u>.

• Dot-matrix printers are <u>slow</u>, <u>noisy</u>, and have <u>poor resolution</u>.
• But they're <u>cheap</u> to run and very <u>reliable</u>.
• And they can print onto <u>long rolls</u> of paper — useful for, say, printing long invoices.

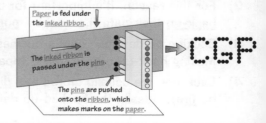

<u>Paper</u> is fed under the <u>inked ribbon</u>.

The <u>inked ribbon</u> is passed under the <u>pins</u>.

The <u>pins</u> are pushed onto the <u>ribbon</u>, which makes marks on the <u>paper</u>.

Nowadays, dot-matrix printers are only really used for printing <u>till receipts</u> and <u>ATM statements</u>.

Get me a printer with a laser on its head...

If you want your <u>electronic data</u> put onto <u>paper</u>, you're going to need a printer. The type of printer that'll suit you best depends on <u>how much</u> printing you need to do, and the level of print <u>quality</u> you need.

More Output Devices

Output isn't just about printing onto paper. Here are some different types of output device. Yes!

Monitors are the Most Common Output Device

1) The monitors used by businesses depend on the type of work being carried out. For example, design work needs large, clear screens.

2) More straightforward work like word processing or entering data into a database can be done on cheaper, smaller screens with a lower resolution.

3) Monitors have changed over the years. In the old days, all monitors used a cathode-ray tube — these monitors were really heavy, took up loads of space on a desk and could damage your eyes.

4) Most computers these days have LCD flat screens. These take up less space on desks and are lightweight — making them easier to move. They also have low power consumption. However, they're easier to damage.

LCD Projectors Make Presentations Much Easier

1) LCD projectors are another type of output device. They can be connected to a laptop or desktop computer.

2) Whatever appears on the computer monitor is projected onto a screen so that it can be viewed by an audience.

3) They're used for training, sales presentations and meetings.

Advantages of LCD Projectors

1) Video images can be displayed. (In fact, they can display anything a normal computer screen can.)

2) Fairly light and portable.

Disadvantages of LCD Projectors

1) Can be quite delicate and easy to break.

2) Need a screen to project images onto.

3) Need dimly lit conditions (not always convenient).

Speakers Output Sound

Speakers are used to output audio (sound, to you and me).

1) Most computers come with speakers built in, but they may not be very good quality. New speakers can usually be connected to improve sound quality or volume.

2) Speakers are needed for audio-conferencing and video-conferencing (see p46) — they allow people's voices to be heard during the meeting.

3) Computers usually have sockets for headphones, too — useful if the user needs privacy, or needs to work quietly (e.g. using a laptop on a train).

Alright — let's rock this sales conference.

Different Output Devices Have Different Functions

The choice of output device will depend on the situation.

1) For example, while writing a letter, you'll probably view it on a monitor so you can see changes instantly.

2) But once you've finished the letter, you might need to print it out and post it.

3) For a presentation, a projector may be best (so the audience won't have to gather round a small screen).

Need audio output? Speakers would be a sound idea...

The development of the LCD projector means that the days of training sessions descending into chaos as dull corporate slides appear upside down will soon be a thing of the past. More's the pity.

Keeping Data Secure

All businesses face threats to their data's security. This includes traditional burglars breaking in and stealing their computers, and more modern criminals who like to commit their crimes electronically...

It's Vital to Keep Business Data Secure

Lots of business data is confidential (e.g. personal or financial data). This needs to be kept safe.

1) Stolen data can be used to commit identity theft, or steal money from bank accounts and credit cards.

2) Some data could reduce a firm's competitiveness if it leaked out to competitors.

3) Data that's been corrupted or altered by unauthorised users is useless to a business.

Physical Security Means Locks and Alarms

1) One type of security risk is having equipment and data physically stolen from buildings.

2) A decent alarm system and quality locks should be used in buildings where valuable equipment and data are stored.

Access Security Involves Usernames and Passwords

Unauthorised access to data (by people inside the firm, or hackers from outside) is potentially very serious.

1) All authorised users of a network should be given usernames and create their own passwords. This will limit unauthorised access to the network.

And users should change their password frequently to be on the safe side.

2) If people leave their computers for a short time, screen-savers (especially ones that need a password before the computer can be used again) can prevent people seeing what's displayed on the screen.

3) A firewall is a software application that increases the protection of a network from external threats. It works by examining all the traffic moving through a network, and denying access to unauthorised users (e.g. hackers). Firewalls increase security, but they can't provide total protection.

4) Encryption software converts data into the form of a code — a key (similar to a password) is needed to decode the data and read it. So even if someone does gain access to your data, as long as they don't know the key, the data won't make any sense. Also, whenever data is transmitted anywhere (e.g. over the internet), there's a risk that it might be 'captured' by baddies — encryption stops it being read.

Spam, Spyware, Viruses — Dangerous and/or Annoying

Malware (malicious software) means any software that's been designed to damage a computer system or its data. You need to know about different kinds, and how a business can protect itself against them.

1) A virus is a program that can corrupt files and even operating systems. Viruses can copy themselves and spread to other computer systems by attaching themselves to emails. Anti-virus software reduces the risks. But it's important to download updates regularly — new viruses are detected practically every day.

2) Spam emails (electronic junk mail) take up storage space, and checking through them wastes time for staff. Anti-spam software tries to detect junk mail, and block it from an inbox.

3) Similarly, anti-adware can help to block unwanted pop-up advertisements.

4) Spyware is software that collects information about the user without their knowledge. It can also install unwanted software and change settings. Anti-spyware packages help to defend computers against it.

Spam — it's a meaty security problem...

It's not hard to see why security is important to businesses — they have a lot to lose if their data is stolen. Okay... normal drill... learn the stuff, then write down what you can remember about potential threats to a business's data and what a business can do to prevent problems. If you get anything wrong, do it again.

Data Protection and the Law

Businesses and other organisations <u>keep data</u> on customers, patients, students and other individuals — whether on paper or on computer files. There are <u>laws</u> to <u>control</u> how the data is used.

The <u>Data Protection Act Controls</u> How Data is Kept and Used

The <u>Data Protection Act (1998)</u> basically says two things...

1) Any <u>business</u> or <u>organisation</u> that holds personal data about <u>individuals</u> ("data subjects") must comply with the <u>8 data protection principles</u> below.

2) Data subjects have various rights to <u>see</u>, <u>correct</u> and prevent their personal data being <u>processed</u> or used for <u>marketing</u> without their permission.

There are <u>Eight Principles</u> of Data Protection

1 Data must not be processed unless there is a <u>specific lawful reason</u> to do so.

E.g., a firm would be able to <u>check</u> if someone usually pays back money on time — that's legal.

2 Data can only be obtained and <u>used for specified purposes</u>.

E.g., businesses can use names and addresses to deliver goods — but if they want to use the data for <u>advertising</u> in the future, they have to ask the data subject's <u>permission</u>.

3 Data should be <u>adequate</u>, <u>relevant</u> and <u>not excessive</u> for the specified use.

E.g., if a business needs to deliver goods, they <u>shouldn't</u> ask for someone's national insurance number.

4 Data must be <u>accurate</u> and <u>kept up to date</u>.

E.g., an employee's examination results must be <u>updated</u> each time they sit extra exams — otherwise incorrect information could be given in a <u>reference</u> to another college or potential employer.

5 Data should <u>not</u> be <u>kept longer than is necessary</u> for the specified purpose.

But this will be different depending on <u>why</u> the data is being kept. E.g., <u>financial</u> information can be kept by certain institutions for up to seven years, but <u>medical</u> records are kept for the life of a patient.

6 Data processing should meet the <u>legal rights</u> of the data subjects (see below).

E.g., some information must not be <u>passed on</u> without the permission of the data subject.

7 Data holders must <u>protect</u> the data <u>against loss, theft or corruption</u>.

It's the duty of the business to <u>back up</u> data, and to dispose of it properly when no longer needed.

8 Data should not be <u>transferred</u> abroad, except to certain other <u>European countries</u>.

This is so that businesses can't just send data <u>abroad</u> to a country where the Data Protection Act doesn't apply.

The Data Protection Act (1998) gives these rights to <u>data subjects</u>:

1) The right to <u>view data</u> held about them (but they must give notice and maybe pay a small fee).
2) The right to <u>prevent</u> the processing of data if it might cause <u>distress or damage</u> to themselves.
3) The right to <u>compensation</u> if damage or distress has been caused.
4) The right to have any inaccurate data <u>changed</u> or <u>deleted</u>.
5) The right to <u>prevent</u> data being used to send <u>junk mail</u>.

The processing of my exam results data has caused distress and damage to myself. If only I'd revised the Data Protection Act... *Sob*

Data Protection — easier than 'gator protection...

There are a few exceptions to the Data Protection Act — e.g. data used for <u>national security</u> purposes, <u>solving crime</u>, or for <u>tax assessment</u> is exempt from some of the data protection principles. The Data Protection Act means data must be stored and used carefully. It means my bank couldn't tell the government how much I spend on hair products every month. Not unless it became a case of national security, that is.

Revision Summary for Section Three

You've made it through to the last page of the section, so why not take a well-earned break?
I'll amuse myself by dumming my fingers on the table till you get back.

Tippity-tap-tap tap-tip-tappity-tip tappity-tap. Tap-tip-tip-tip-tappity-tip-tap-tap.

Back so soon? Well, you're going to like this — a whole heap of questions about ICT data systems.
Thought you'd be pleased. Do some finger-drumming before you start if you like — it's a free country.

1) What's the difference between primary and secondary data sources?
2) Explain the main features of paper-based and computer-based systems.
   Give some advantages and disadvantages of each type of system.
3) What is meant by 'hardware'? And 'software'?
4) Describe the main pros and cons of: a) a desktop PC   b) a laptop PC.
5) What is meant by 'input device'?
6) Give one advantage and one disadvantage of a QWERTY keyboard.
7) Explain what a concept keyboard is, and give an example of a business that might use one.
8) Give two situations where a joystick might be used.
9) What does EPOS stand for? What do EPOS systems do, and where are they usually used?
10) Give one benefit and one drawback of voice-recognition systems.
11) Explain the differences between manual data forms and electronic data forms.
12) What's the difference between internal and external storage devices? Give one example of each.
13) Give two benefits and two drawbacks of memory sticks.
14) Explain the differences between CD-ROMS, CD-Rs and CD-RWs.
15) What advantages do DVDs have over CDs?
16) Why should firms always create back-up copies of their data?
17) Why might businesses want to store data at a different site?
18) Explain the differences between laser, ink-jet and dot-matrix printers.
    What types of business might want to use each of these types of printer?
19) Describe what an LCD projector does, and when you might use one.
20) Give three reasons why firms need to keep their data secure.
21) What does physical security protect against? Give two examples of physical security measures.
22) Explain three things that can be done to protect data on a network of computers.
23) Explain what the following security threats are, and name the software that protects against them.
        a) Spam;   b) Spyware;   c) Viruses.
24) What does the Data Protection Act control?
25) Explain the eight principles of Data Protection.
26) What five rights do data subjects have under the Data Protection Act?
27) Give two examples of data that may not be covered by the Data Protection Act.

Patterns of Work

You need to know about different types of contracts of employment.
To be more specific, you need to know about permanent, temporary, part-time and full-time work.

Employment Can be Full Time or Part Time...

1) Working full time usually means around 35-40 hours a week.
   Part-time staff work 'less than a full working week' — usually between 10-30 hours per week.

2) Some people prefer to have a full-time job, or need to work full time for financial reasons.
   Other people choose to work part time, so they can spend more time with family or on other interests.
   Or they may only be able to work part time because of other commitments.
   Many businesses are now more flexible about letting staff work around their family lives (see p16).

3) There are pros and cons for businesses. Full-time staff are good if there's enough work for them to do.
   But employing staff part time can make sense if a business is only really busy at certain periods.

> • In 1997, the law was changed to give part-time and full-time workers equal employment rights.
>   (Before then, part-time workers weren't entitled to all the benefits that full-time workers were.)
>
> • As a result, employees in the UK are now more willing to take on part-time positions.

...and Permanent or Temporary

1) A permanent contract of employment has no end date. The person stays at the firm unless:
   (i) they choose to leave,   (ii) they're dismissed for misconduct,   (iii) their job is made redundant.

Welcome aboard. We'll let you know each evening whether you'll have a job the next day.

2) A temporary contract is for a fixed period (e.g. six months, one year, or whatever). At the end of the period, the contract can be renewed, or the person can leave the company.

3) Temporary contracts can make it easier for the firm to employ people with particular skills for a particular period (without the commitment of a permanent contract). This can make it easier to adjust the number of staff employed according to the circumstances of the business.

4) The main problem for temporary workers is that they often have a less stable income. This can make it more difficult to get loans or a mortgage.

All Employees Have a Contract of Employment

All employees have a contract of employment — a legal agreement between the employee and the employer. This can be verbal or written. However, most employers must give employees the following information in writing within two months of starting work:

- the job title (or a brief job description)
- the starting date of the employment (and the end date for a temporary employee)
- the hours of work, the starting pay and the regular date of payment
- where the employee will be working

- the holiday the employee's entitled to
- details of sickness pay and any company pension scheme
- information about disciplinary procedures
- the length of notice the employee has to give if they want to leave

But really, isn't everything temporary...

One day, the Universe might start to collapse in on itself under gravity and shrink back into a tiny speck. But don't worry about that for now — you just need to know the differences between various employment contracts, and the main features of these contracts. You can work out how to save the universe later.

Recruitment — Job Analysis

Recruitment is about appointing the <u>best person</u> to do the job. A business needs to understand <u>what the job will involve</u> so that it can decide what the right person <u>will be like</u>.

The Job Description Says What the Job Involves

1) The job description is a <u>written description</u> of what the job consists of. It includes the <u>formal title</u> of the job, its main <u>purpose</u>, its <u>main duties</u> and any <u>occasional duties</u>.

2) It also includes details of who the job holder will <u>report to</u> and whether they're responsible for <u>managing</u> other staff. It may include some <u>performance targets</u>.

3) Without a job description it would be impossible to write the <u>person specification</u>...

> **The Necks Directory Ltd. — Job Description**
> Job Title: Full-time Vampire Operative.
> Reports to: Vampire Team Leader.
> Responsible for: Trainee Vampire Operatives.
> Main purpose of job: To climb through people's windows at night and suck their nourishing blood.
> Duties and Responsibilities:
> — to bite the necks of humans while they sleep;
> — to wear a large black cape and cackle menacingly;
> — to meet neck-biting targets set by Vampire Team Leader;
> — may involve occasional travel to Whitby for meetings.

The Person Specification Describes the Ideal Person

> **Vampire Operative — Person Specification**
> Essential: 5 GCSEs including Business Studies, NVQ Anatomy Level 3.
> Desirable: Two years of vampiring experience.
> Skills: Ability to climb through windows, bite necks, turn into a bat etc. Good communication skills.
> Attitudes: Fear of daylight, willingness to work unsocial hours, must enjoy meeting new people.

1) The person specification lists the <u>qualifications</u>, <u>experience</u>, <u>skills</u> and <u>personal qualities</u> needed for the job.

2) They are sometimes divided into:
   - <u>essential</u> criteria — things the candidate <u>must</u> have, and
   - <u>desirable</u> criteria — things the candidate would <u>ideally</u> have.

See next page for more about skills and attitudes.

The Job Can Be Advertised Internally or Externally

1) The purpose of a job advert is to get <u>as many suitable people</u> as possible to apply for the job.

2) The advert should <u>describe the job</u> and the <u>skills</u> required. It will often state what the <u>pay</u> is, and what <u>training</u> and <u>other benefits</u> are offered. It must explain <u>how</u> the person should apply for the job.

3) The firm can decide to advertise the job <u>internally</u> or <u>externally</u>:

Internal Advertising
- When advertising <u>internally</u>, adverts are usually put up on <u>noticeboards</u> or sent round to staff.
- It's much <u>cheaper</u>, the post can be filled <u>more quickly</u>, and the candidates will already <u>know a lot</u> about the firm.
- On the <u>downside</u>, there will be <u>no 'new blood' or ideas</u>, and the promotion will leave a <u>vacancy</u> to fill.

External Advertising
- If the job is advertised <u>externally</u>, the advert will be seen by <u>more people</u>.
- Possible locations include local and national <u>newspapers</u>, <u>job centres</u>, <u>trade journals</u> and <u>employment agencies</u>.
- Advertising in the national press is <u>expensive</u>, so firms may only do that for specialist jobs.
- The firm may also advertise the job on their own <u>website</u>, or on the websites of <u>agencies</u>.

Lonely business WLTM right person for ~~cuddles~~ hard graft...

Recruitment is like love. You decide what <u>type of person</u> you're looking for, and the features you find most <u>desirable</u>. Then you put an <u>advert</u> in the newspaper and prepare for disappointment. Exactly like love, right?

Recruitment — The Selection Process

The <u>selection process</u> happens after the job has been advertised. All the candidates' <u>applications</u> are looked at and employers create a <u>short list</u> of the people they want to <u>interview</u> in person. Here's how it's done...

Candidates Apply with a Written Application...

A <u>written application</u> helps firms to decide which candidates match the <u>person specification</u>.

1) A <u>curriculum vitae (CV)</u> is a summary of a person's personal details, skills, qualifications, experience and interests (p42). It's designed to give the firm the basic <u>facts</u>. Almost <u>all</u> employers ask for a CV.

2) An <u>application form</u> is designed by the firm and filled in by the applicant. It gives the firm the information it wants — and nothing else. This makes it easier to <u>compare</u> applications.

Some firms also ask for a <u>letter of application</u> — these allow candidates to <u>choose</u> what they want to say. They're more <u>personal</u>, but <u>harder to compare</u>.

3) Most businesses now accept <u>electronic versions</u> of <u>written applications</u>. Some even have <u>online</u> application forms.

...Which Helps the Firm to Make a Short List

I'm really getting this short-list narrowed down.

Candidates are usually <u>short-listed</u> in the following way:

1) Each candidate's application is <u>read</u> — sometimes by more than one person.

2) The application is <u>compared</u> to the <u>job description</u> and <u>person specification</u>. Any <u>essential</u> or <u>desirable characteristics</u> met by the candidate are recorded.

> A <u>good application</u> will be <u>to the point</u> and <u>refer</u> to skills and qualities mentioned in the <u>job description</u> and <u>person specification</u>. ✓

> A <u>bad application</u> might be <u>waffly</u>, <u>inaccurate</u>, not contain enough information or be <u>poorly written</u>. ✗

3) The employers also look for a <u>balance</u> of <u>skills</u> and <u>attitudes</u>:

> **SKILLS** are things a person has <u>learnt</u> (such as being able to program a computer).
> **ATTITUDES** are <u>personal qualities</u> a person has (such as being able to work in a team).

> A <u>highly skilled</u> person should be good at <u>technical</u> tasks. But they may cause <u>problems</u> for other reasons — e.g. not cooperating with other staff or demanding higher pay.

> A candidate with a <u>good attitude</u> may <u>fit in</u> better. But they might need extra <u>skills training</u>.

4) The candidates who seem to have the <u>right qualities</u>, <u>skills</u> and <u>attitudes</u> to do the job are included on a <u>short list</u>. These people are usually then invited to an <u>interview</u>.

Employers Meet Short-Listed Candidates in Interviews

1) Written applications are great for narrowing down a list of job candidates. But people can <u>exaggerate</u> in CVs and application forms, and they don't give much idea of what the candidate is like <u>in person</u>. That's why face-to-face <u>interviews</u> are really important when recruiting new staff.

2) Interviews are used to assess a candidate's <u>confidence</u>, their <u>social</u> and <u>verbal skills</u>, and whether they'll be <u>compatible</u> with existing workers. Businesses also want to find out about the candidate's general <u>attitude</u>.

Sorry. I can never behave naturally at interviews.

3) Some people think that interviews are <u>not a good way</u> to select — people don't behave <u>naturally</u> in a formal interview. The skills needed to be good at interview are often <u>different</u> from the skills needed to do the job.

I'm highly skilled at writing titles that fit neatly into boxes

In your exam, you might be asked to read some applications and <u>judge</u> how <u>suitable</u> each candidate would be for the job. Don't panic — just remember to keep the <u>job description</u> and <u>person specification</u> in mind.

Employment Law

This page is crammed <u>full of facts</u> about the <u>law</u>. Make sure you know what the law <u>says</u>, and understand the <u>impact</u> it has on employers.

① Contracts of Employment and the Minimum Wage

1) Within <u>two months</u> of starting work, most employees must be told <u>in writing</u> information about pay, hours they're expected to work, holidays, pension schemes, and so on (see p29 for more information).

2) All staff should also have a copy of the firm's <u>discipline procedure</u>. This explains which offences would lead to a <u>warning</u>, and which would lead to <u>dismissal</u>.

3) The Government sets a <u>national minimum wage</u> for all workers, depending on their age. This means businesses can't cut costs on their wage bills by paying workers <u>less</u> than the legal minimum.

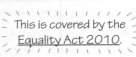
This is covered by the Equality Act 2010.

② Anti-Discrimination Law

1) Employers must not <u>discriminate</u> against employees or candidates for employment on the basis of:

- gender,
- ethnicity,
- disabilities,
- age,
- sexual orientation,
- religion.

This is covered by the Equality Act 2010.

2) For example, employers might need to <u>adapt</u> the workplace for people with <u>disabilities</u> (e.g. install adapted toilets). And women must be paid the same as men doing the <u>same job</u> for the same employer.

③ Leaving Employment

1) Employees are also protected against <u>unfair dismissal</u>. This means that firms need a <u>good reason</u> for dismissing staff.

This is covered by the Equality Act 2010.

2) This could be because they're <u>incompetent</u>, or are guilty of <u>gross misconduct</u>.

3) Employees can only be made <u>redundant</u> if the job they're employed to do <u>no longer exists</u> (e.g. if <u>machines</u> can now do the same job). The firm <u>cannot re-advertise</u> a redundant job.

4) Employees who think they have been <u>unfairly</u> dismissed or made redundant can usually appeal to an <u>employment tribunal</u>. The tribunal can award <u>compensation</u> or <u>reinstate</u> the employee.

The Law Aims to Give Employees a Fair Deal

1) The Equality Act (2010) is designed to make sure that staff are treated <u>fairly</u>.

2) The law can cause <u>problems</u> for businesses. For example, it can be <u>expensive</u> and <u>time consuming</u> to keep up to date with new legislation. And firms may also have to go through <u>costly court cases</u> to prove that they've behaved legally (and be <u>fined</u> if they haven't).

3) But treating staff <u>fairly</u> means they'll be <u>happier</u> and better <u>motivated</u>. They'll also be more likely to stay with the firm for longer (which saves money on <u>recruiting</u> and <u>training</u> new staff).

All staff are equal — but some more equal than others...

Newsflash: the staff of a business are <u>human beings</u>. This means they'll be <u>happier</u> if they're treated <u>fairly</u>. I guess it's a bit sad that a <u>law</u> is needed to enforce a bit of basic fairness between people, but there you go.

Staff Training

Training is the main way that a firm <u>invests</u> in its <u>employees</u>. This page covers three basic types of training. And guess what... you need to be able to <u>judge</u> which type would be <u>most suitable</u> in a given situation.

① Induction Training is for New Staff

1) Induction training <u>introduces</u> the new employee to their workplace, and should help to make the new employee feel <u>welcome</u>.

2) It includes introducing them to their <u>fellow workers</u> and advising them of <u>company rules</u> — including health and safety rules. They should also be given a <u>tour</u> of the site so they don't get lost. It may also include initial training on how to do their new job.

② On-the-Job Training is Learning by Doing

Yeah, we're supposed to lock the safe every night, but we never actually bother.

1) This is the <u>most common</u> form of training. The employee learns to do their job better by being <u>shown how to do it</u>, and then <u>practising</u>. It's also sometimes called <u>internal training</u> (as it's handled within the business).

2) It's <u>cost-effective</u> for the employer because the employee <u>works</u> and <u>learns</u> at the same time.

3) A problem is that the training is often <u>given by colleagues</u> — so <u>bad working practices</u> can be passed on.

③ Off-the-Job Training Can be Internal or External

1) Off-the-job training happens when staff learn <u>away</u> from their workplace.

2) If the firm has its own <u>training department</u>, it can still be done <u>internally</u>. Training given by <u>other organisations</u> (e.g. college courses) is called <u>external training</u>.

3) It's more <u>expensive</u> than on-the-job training, and sometimes not as <u>directly related</u> to the actual job. But it's often <u>higher quality</u> because it's taught by people who are better <u>qualified</u> to train others.

4) It's best used when <u>introducing new skills</u> or training people for <u>promotion</u>.

Training Benefits Both the Employer and the Employee

Benefits of training to employers

1) Trained staff should be <u>better</u> at their jobs, which should mean they're more <u>efficient</u> and <u>productive</u>.

2) Training can give staff the skills to do <u>new jobs</u> within the company. This may <u>save</u> time and money on advertising the jobs <u>externally</u>.

3) Training can help staff stay <u>up to date</u> with <u>changes</u> in the business.

4) Staff may feel like they're <u>progressing</u> in the firm, which might make them <u>stay</u> with the firm for <u>longer</u> (which will save on recruitment costs).

Benefits of training to employees

1) Employees with up-to-date <u>knowledge</u> and <u>skills</u> should be able to do their jobs better with fewer problems — which often increases <u>job satisfaction</u> and <u>motivation</u>.

2) Over time, gaining new skills may mean that they can be <u>promoted</u> to jobs with <u>better pay</u> and <u>more responsibility</u>.

3) They may also be able to get better jobs with <u>other businesses</u>. Staff can take advantage of training to help them meet their <u>career ambitions</u>.

It's training, men — hallelujah...

The different types of training on this page are all used for slightly different purposes. But the <u>end result</u> should be <u>the same</u> for them all — well trained staff who are <u>more motivated</u> and <u>productive</u>. Smiley face.

Financial Rewards

Most businesses <u>pay</u> their employees for their work. But these <u>financial rewards</u> can be worked out in different ways. You might need to do some <u>pay calculations</u> in the exam, but they won't be too bad, honest.

If People Do More Work Their Wages Increase...

<u>Wages</u> are paid weekly or monthly — usually to <u>manual workers</u>. Wages are calculated in one of two ways:

At this rate I can make this job last all week...

TIME RATE pays workers by the <u>hour</u>.
- If a painter is paid <u>£6 per hour</u> and works <u>40 hours</u> in a week, their week's wage will be £6 × 40 = <u>£240</u>.
- Time rate encourages people to work <u>long hours</u> — the problem is they also have an incentive to work <u>slowly</u>.
- Time rate is best for jobs where <u>measuring</u> a worker's output is <u>difficult</u> — e.g. a bus driver.

PIECE RATE is often used if a worker's <u>output</u> can be <u>measured</u>.
- Say a worker who sews sleeves onto shirts is paid a piece rate of <u>10p per sleeve</u>. If they sew <u>2000 sleeves</u> per week, their weekly wage will be £0.10 × 2000 = <u>£200</u>.
- Piece rate encourages people to <u>work quickly</u> — this may be a problem if they work so fast that <u>quality</u> starts to suffer.

Here's the formula for calculating total wages using time rate and piece rate:
<u>Total wage = rate × amount of work done</u>

...But a Salary Stays the Same

1) A salary is a <u>fixed</u> amount paid every month. Salaries are usually paid to <u>office staff</u> and <u>management</u> who don't directly help to make the product. A salary of <u>£24,000 per year</u> means you're paid £24,000 ÷ 12 months = <u>£2000 per month</u>.

2) The <u>advantage</u> of a salary is that the business and workers both <u>know exactly</u> how much the pay will be.

3) A disadvantage is that it <u>doesn't link</u> pay directly to <u>performance</u>, so it doesn't encourage employees to <u>work harder</u> to earn more money.

Employers Can Give Staff Extra Payments

1) Some employers pay staff an <u>overtime rate</u> if they work <u>extra hours</u> on top of their normal working week. E.g. a painter who's normally paid £6 an hour might be paid £9 an hour to work at the weekend.

2) With <u>performance-related pay</u> the amount employees <u>earn</u> depends on how well they <u>work</u>.

<u>Commission</u> is paid to sales staff. They earn a <u>small basic salary</u> and then earn more money for every item they <u>sell</u>.

A <u>bonus</u> is a <u>lump sum</u> added to pay, usually once a year. It's paid if the worker has met their <u>performance targets</u>.

3) Some businesses make payments into a <u>pension scheme</u> for employees. Others offer a <u>profit sharing</u> scheme — where a percentage of the company's profits is divided up between employees, for example.

Piece rate — it'll depend on how many cups of tea you drink...

Unless they're volunteers, the main reason that most people work is for the <u>remuneration</u> (i.e. the money), which helps them to avoid starvation. Staff can be paid <u>wages</u> or a <u>salary</u>, depending on their job.

Financial Rewards

Rates of pay can <u>change</u>. Also, money is usually <u>deducted</u> (taken away) from people's pay before they're paid. Yep, I think you know where I'm headed... this is the page with <u>calculations</u> on it.

Changes in Pay are Sometimes Worked Out as Percentages

1) <u>Gross pay</u> is the amount of money an employee is paid — their wage or salary. The amount that an employee gets to <u>keep</u> after <u>deductions</u> (e.g. taxes and pension contributions) is called <u>net pay</u>.

2) Rates of pay can change over time. People may be given <u>pay rises</u>, or paid extra to work <u>overtime</u>. Some deductions and changes in pay are calculated as <u>percentages</u> of gross pay.

Example 1

An employee earns a gross salary of £1600 per month. She pays 3% of her gross salary into a pension fund. How much does she pay into her pension each month?

> You need to work out 3% of £1600.
>
> 1% of £1600 = $\dfrac{£1600}{100}$ = £16
>
> So 3% of £1600 = £16 × 3 = <u>£48 per month</u>

Example 2

A worker earns a time-rate wage of £8 per hour. If he is given a 5% pay rise, calculate his new hourly wage.

> Here, you need to <u>add</u> 5% to the old wage.
>
> 5% of £8 = $\dfrac{£8}{100}$ × 5 = £0.40
>
> So the new hourly wage is £8 + £0.40
> = <u>£8.40 per hour</u>

Fringe Benefits are Extra Perks Given to Employees

<u>Fringe benefits</u> are sometimes given to staff <u>in addition</u> to their pay. For example...

STAFF DISCOUNTS Many businesses offer their staff <u>money off</u> their own products. This <u>saves money</u> for the staff, and <u>discourages</u> them from buying from <u>competing companies</u>.

EMPLOYEE PENSIONS The firm pays a fixed amount into the employee's <u>pension account</u> each month. This money is <u>saved up</u> over the years, ready to be used when the employee <u>retires</u>.

PRIVATE MEDICAL INSURANCE The firm pays for medical <u>insurance policies</u> for its staff. This means that employees can <u>claim back money</u> if they need to pay for private medical treatment.

LIFE INSURANCE This provides <u>financial payments</u> to an employee's family if he or she <u>dies</u> while working for the firm. Again, the company <u>pays</u> for the insurance policy.

Look how cute he is.
Attaboy Henry.

GYM MEMBERSHIP Or free use of other <u>leisure facilities</u>.

DAILY MEAL ALLOWANCE This could mean the employee is <u>compensated</u> for food they've bought while travelling, say. Or it could be free food in a <u>staff canteen</u>.

PRAISE Most staff like it when their boss says something <u>nice</u> about them. And it's <u>free</u>.

Sherlock's pension — it's a brilliant deduction, Holmes...

Unfortunately, there's no direct <u>financial reward</u> for doing well in your GCSEs (unless your dad/aunt/teacher is bribing you with £10 for every exam you pass). But think about all the <u>valuable skills</u> you're gaining. Yep.

Revision Summary for Section Four

Human resources aren't like other resources. Humans have feelings, so they don't like working 100 hours a week in a freezing cold box with no lights and no-one to talk to. Businesses have to treat their employees reasonably well, which can create extra costs — but it's nice when everybody's happy.

Speaking of happiness, here are some questions. Don't come out of your box till you've answered them all.

1) Why might some people choose to work part time? Why might other people need to work full time?
2) Why might a business want to employ workers on temporary contracts?
3) Describe one problem that temporary contracts cause for employees.
4) List eight bits of information that should be included in a contract of employment.
5) What's the main purpose of a job description? What information should it contain?
6) Explain the difference between a job description and a person specification.
7) What information should a job advert include?
8) Give three advantages and two disadvantages of advertising a job internally.
9) Describe the main features of CVs and application forms.
10) What's the difference between skills and attitudes?
11) Give a reason why most firms ask short-listed candidates to an interview.
12) Explain the drawbacks of interviews as a way of selecting candidates.
13) What information is contained in a firm's discipline procedure?
14) It's illegal to discriminate against employees because of their sex.
    Give five other illegal grounds for discrimination.
15) Under what circumstances is it legal to make staff redundant?
16) Explain one problem that employment laws can make for a business.
17) What benefits can employment laws bring to a business?
18) When does induction training take place? What should it include?
19) Give one advantage and one disadvantage each of on-the-job training and off-the-job training.
20) Give four benefits that training staff has for employers.
    Now give three benefits that training can bring to employees.
21) What's the difference between a time rate and a piece rate?
    What kind of work is each rate best suited to?
22) A shop assistant is paid a time rate of £7 per hour. He works 35 hours per week.
    Calculate his weekly wage.
23) Explain the difference between a commission and a bonus.
24) A factory worker is paid a piece rate for packing boxes. Last week, she earned £225.
    This week, she packed 8% more boxes. How much will she earn for this week?
25) Describe seven types of fringe benefits.

24. £243
22. £245

Purposes of Communication

<u>Communication</u>. It's written in big letters on the front of this book. But what actually <u>is</u> it...

Communication Involves the <u>Exchange of Information</u>

1) Communication involves <u>transmitting</u> (sending) information from a <u>sender</u> to a <u>receiver</u>. The information that's sent is called the <u>message</u>.

2) Messages are sent using a particular <u>medium</u>. Examples of media include: email, letter, phone...

One <u>medium</u>, but two <u>media</u> etc.

3) The <u>receiver</u> of the message can send <u>feedback</u> to show they've received it and <u>understood</u> it. Feedback is important for judging how <u>successful</u> the communication has been.

<u>Before</u> <u>Sending</u> a Message, You Need to <u>Choose</u> a <u>System</u>

The <u>main</u> things that will decide how a message is sent are...

1 <u>Who</u> the sender and receiver are, and the <u>relationship</u> between them.

2 What <u>information</u> the message contains.

3 The <u>purpose</u> of the message (i.e. the <u>reason</u> for sending it).

Based on these factors, the sender will <u>choose</u> the best <u>communication system</u> for sending the message. A communication system is made up of a <u>method</u>, a <u>channel</u> and a <u>medium</u> of communication.

Choose the Best <u>Method</u> of Communication

Methods

WRITTEN messages can be kept and read <u>many times</u>, so they're good for <u>complex information</u>.

ORAL messages are <u>spoken</u> — they're more <u>personal</u>, and good for getting <u>immediate feedback</u>.

VISUAL methods involve <u>images</u> or <u>body language</u> — they express meaning <u>quickly</u> without words.
- <u>Pictorial</u> methods use <u>pictures</u> (e.g. ☺ is a quick, informal way to express happiness).
- <u>Graphical</u> methods use <u>graphs</u>, <u>charts</u> and <u>diagrams</u> to show <u>technical information</u> and data.

Choose the Right <u>Channel</u> of Communication

Types of channel

Internal and external — Messages that <u>don't leave</u> the business go through <u>internal</u> channels. Messages sent to receivers <u>outside</u> the firm are sent through <u>external</u> channels.

Formal and informal — <u>Formal</u> channels are used for <u>official business</u> (e.g. formal letters sent to suppliers, or job applicants). <u>Informal</u> channels are <u>less official</u> — e.g. <u>word-of-mouth</u> messages.

Confidential and non-confidential — Confidential messages (e.g. financial data) need to be <u>private</u>.

Urgent and non-urgent — Urgent channels are used to deliver <u>important</u> messages <u>quickly</u>.

Choose the Best <u>Medium</u>

The medium means the '<u>equipment</u>' you use to send the message — this will <u>depend</u> on the <u>method</u> and the <u>channels</u> of communication.

You will choose the best medium...

Communication system addict — I never can get enough...*

Okay, so there's a lot of <u>jargon</u> on this page (see p39 for more about that, by the way). Sadly, you'll need to use these technical terms to talk about <u>how communication works</u>. It may seem weird now, but bear with me — the rest of the pages in this section should make it clearer what all this actually <u>means</u>.

*Another bang-up-to-date pop music reference from CGP.

Internal and External Communication

Good communication is <u>good</u>. Bad communication is <u>bad</u>. Easy so far. Now for the details...

Internal Communication Happens Inside the Firm

Internal communication can be between <u>different</u> layers of a hierarchy, or between people on the <u>same level</u>.

> Communication between <u>different layers</u> of the hierarchy:
> - <u>Managers</u> and <u>supervisors</u> need to communicate with <u>operatives</u> to give them tasks.
> - Operatives can give <u>feedback</u> to their managers.
>
> Communication across the <u>same level</u> of the hierarchy:
> - Team members need to <u>exchange information</u> to complete tasks effectively.
> - Different departments need to communicate with each other to <u>coordinate</u> their activities.

Hierarchies are covered on p10.

1) The <u>media</u> staff use to communicate (e.g. email, telephone, meetings) may depend on their positions in the company. For example, not everyone may have access to a computer.

Future Plans
- Improve service.
- Replace all junior staff with robots.

I feel more motivated already.

2) <u>Good</u> internal communication means <u>staff</u> will be <u>better informed</u> about what's going on in the firm, improving their <u>motivation</u>. Communication between staff should also mean that they <u>work together better</u> and make <u>fewer mistakes</u>. These things should increase <u>efficiency</u>, <u>productivity</u>, and levels of <u>customer service</u>. An efficient business with happy customers should make <u>more profit</u>.

3) <u>Poor</u> internal communication can lead to employees feeling <u>alienated</u> — that their opinions are <u>misunderstood</u> or <u>ignored</u>. This isn't good for staff <u>morale</u>, <u>productivity</u>, the <u>company</u>, or its <u>customers</u> — profits could suffer.

External Communication is With People Outside the Firm

1) Businesses need to exchange information with a <u>wide range</u> of <u>stakeholders</u> in the outside world.

> - Businesses communicate with their <u>suppliers</u> to agree the size, cost and delivery dates of orders.
> - Businesses communicate with their <u>customers</u> in order to <u>improve sales</u>. E.g. <u>market research</u> to find out what customers want, and <u>advertising</u> to promote their products. <u>Customer care</u> is also important — e.g. dealing with complaints and questions about products.
> - Customers can also provide <u>feedback</u> — e.g. by filling in <u>questionnaires</u>, or phoning a <u>helpline</u>.

2) When communicating with external receivers, firms need to make sure that the messages they send are delivered in an <u>appropriate form</u> for each type of receiver (as well as being <u>clear</u> and <u>accurate</u>).

3) Businesses also need to think carefully about the <u>image</u> (see p47) they want to create for themselves.

> For example, the firm might take part in <u>environmental</u> schemes. Or the firm might do something to benefit the <u>local community</u>. If people are <u>aware</u> of this, it might generate trust and good will.

4) Good communication with customers is vital if a business is having a <u>problem</u>. For example, if a company won't be able to deliver something <u>on time</u>, it's usually best to tell the customer. If the customer knows the delivery will be late, they can make other plans instead of waiting in for something to arrive.

Okay... Father Christmas calling to say that he'd be late was never going to end well.

5) Bad external communication can cause <u>misunderstandings</u>, which could be pretty serious. For example, <u>suppliers</u> might deliver goods late (or the wrong goods) if they've misunderstood an order. Similarly, <u>customers</u> will be upset if their orders are delivered late, or if they feel they're not being listened to.

Thumping people you don't like = bad communication...

Poor communication can have a big impact on businesses — inefficient, badly-motivated employees and dissatisfied customers are likely to result in <u>fewer sales</u>, <u>less profit</u> and <u>conflict</u> with stakeholders.

Barriers to Communication

So... you know what information you want to communicate, and how you're going to send the message. But there are still factors that can affect the receiver's interpretation — you need to keep these in mind, too...

Barriers Can Prevent Good Communication

Just choose a vector space with an orthogonal basis, then apply Fourier analysis to derive the system's non-trivial roots.

Yessir.

- ⊖ **JARGON** — this is technical language to do with a particular subject. People who aren't experts in that subject may <u>not understand</u>.

- ⊖ **NOISE** — this could be <u>traffic</u> noise making it <u>hard to hear</u> a phone call. Or it might be <u>visual noise</u> — e.g. <u>too much information</u> on a page can make it hard to pick out the important points.

- ⊖ **POOR CHOICE OF CHANNEL OR MEDIUM** — e.g. an <u>urgent</u> letter sent by <u>second-class</u> post may not get there in time. And complex information might be best <u>written down</u>, rather than spoken, so that the receiver doesn't <u>forget</u> any of it.

- ⊖ **INAPPROPRIATE PRESENTATION** — a message's presentation should be <u>suitable</u> for the audience. E.g. an advert should be easy to <u>understand</u> — if it's <u>too complex</u>, customers might <u>lose interest</u>.

- ⊖ **EMOTIONAL INTERFERENCE** — e.g. if the sender and the receiver don't get on personally, it can affect how the communication is <u>understood</u>.

- ⊖ **TRUST AND HONESTY** — if the receiver thinks the sender is <u>dishonest</u>, they may be <u>suspicious</u> about the content of the message.

- ⊖ **CULTURAL DIFFERENCES** — communicating <u>internationally</u> can be tricky. <u>Foreign languages</u> can easily be <u>mistranslated</u>. Also, what seems <u>polite</u> in one country may be <u>rude</u> in another.

- ⊖ **THE STATUS OF THE SENDER** People outside a business are often more likely to <u>trust</u> information if it comes from somebody who's <u>high up</u> in the organisation.

Checking Documents for Errors is a Good Idea

<u>Errors</u> can also be a barrier to communication — they can make messages <u>misleading</u> and <u>confusing</u>. Luckily, written and visual messages can be <u>checked</u> for errors <u>before</u> they're sent.

1) **Errors in spelling, punctuation and grammar** — In formal business documents, this looks <u>unprofessional</u> — the firm may <u>lose respect</u> if words aren't spelt <u>correctly</u>.

2) **Errors in tone** — This will depend on the sender, message and receiver. A <u>formal</u> business letter to a customer needs formal <u>language</u>. If the tone is too chatty, it can seem <u>disrespectful</u>.

3) **Factual errors** — <u>Factual errors</u> can cause big problems — e.g. putting the wrong prices in a catalogue could damage a firm's reputation. Giving out misleading information could even be a <u>criminal offence</u>.

4) **Problems with graphics and diagrams** — Graphics are supposed to make information <u>clearer</u>. But if they're not properly labelled, they could just add to the <u>confusion</u>.

- Checking business documents for errors can save <u>embarrassment</u>, <u>confusion</u>, and more <u>serious problems</u>.

- The main drawback of checking for mistakes is that it takes <u>time</u> and <u>money</u> to do it properly. But it's usually time and money <u>well spent</u>.

My Barry's Barrier than your Barry...

When sending a message, it's important to think about how the receiver will <u>interpret</u> it — if the message is <u>unclear</u>, <u>confusing</u>, or full of <u>mistakes</u>, your point might come not across the way you <u>meant</u> it to. Capisce?

Written Communication — Letters

Written communication is massively important to businesses. Once a message is written down on paper, you can <u>read it again and again</u> until your fingers have worn away the ink and your eyes have shrivelled up like walnuts inside your skull. <u>Business letters</u> are a very common form of written communication.

Business Letters are Used for External Communication

1) <u>Letters</u> are one of the main ways that businesses communicate <u>externally</u>.
   They're sometimes used for <u>formal internal</u> communication as well. They're used when:

   - A <u>formal message</u> is needed — e.g. to confirm an order with a supplier.
   - A <u>permanent record</u> of the message is needed — e.g. if the terms of a contract are being changed.
   - A message is <u>complicated</u> or a <u>lot of information</u> needs to be given.

2) Formal business letters are usually presented in a <u>standard format</u>. There's <u>no need</u> for flashy graphics, just neatly presented text that uses straightforward formal language to <u>get the facts across</u>.

   > Some firms also send <u>informal</u> letters to <u>promote</u> products and special offers. The idea with these letters is that customers will be encouraged to make <u>more purchases</u> if the firm seems <u>friendly</u> and <u>trustworthy</u>.

3) <u>Word-processed</u> letters can be <u>mail-merged</u>. This means that very similar letters can be sent to <u>large numbers</u> of individual receivers, with their personal details slotted in automatically.

   Mail merge makes it easy for firms to send out <u>thousands</u> of letters, even if customers <u>haven't asked</u> for them — it's often seen as <u>junk mail</u>.

   See p59-60 for more about business letters and mail merge.

Sending a Letter has Benefits and Drawbacks

Benefits of business letters

1) The business can keep a <u>copy</u> of a letter it sends (either electronically, on paper, or both). This can be used as <u>proof</u> that the message has been <u>sent</u> and of what the message <u>said</u>.

2) Both the sender and receiver can keep the letter and use it for <u>future reference</u>. This can be helpful if the information is important or complicated.

3) The business can get proof that the message was <u>delivered</u> if they use <u>recorded delivery</u>. <u>Fax machines</u> (see p43) also give receipts to show that a faxed letter has been received.

Wish I'd used mail merge...

Drawbacks of business letters

1) Posted letters take <u>at least a day</u> to be delivered — so they're <u>not suitable</u> for <u>urgent messages</u>. Faxing a letter is much quicker though.

2) Posted letters can get <u>lost</u> or <u>stolen</u> in the post. There are more <u>secure</u> channels you can use (e.g. Royal Mail's Special Delivery™ service), but these are <u>more expensive</u>.

3) The sender gets <u>no immediate feedback</u> from the reader.

Business — a mail-dominated world...

Business letters are perfect for <u>formal</u> communication, but they're <u>not</u> usually very <u>eye-catching</u>. If a firm really wants to dazzle its <u>customers</u>, it may be better to use a more <u>visual</u> method, like a <u>flyer</u> or a <u>brochure</u> (see p42). Learn when business letters are used, and what makes a good business letter. Got it? Good.

Internal Written Communication

Employees of a business often like to write <u>internal</u> messages to each other.
It means there's a <u>written record</u> of the information, and it can be an effective way to communicate.

Memo *is Short for* Memorandum

1) A memorandum (or '<u>memo</u>') is a <u>formal written message</u> (printed on <u>paper</u>) sent to people <u>inside</u> an organisation. Nowadays, emails are often sent where memos were used in the past. But a memo is more formal than an email (it can even seem a bit 'stuffy').

2) The main <u>advantage</u> of memos is that there's a <u>hard copy</u> of the message that can be kept.

3) But emails are <u>quicker</u> and don't use any <u>paper</u>.

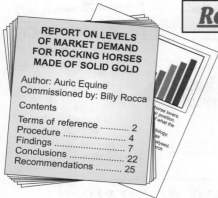

Reports *are Written After* Investigations

1) <u>Reports</u> are written when somebody has been asked (or <u>commissioned</u>) to <u>investigate</u> a topic and give detailed <u>advice</u> and <u>recommendations</u>.

2) Written reports usually follow a <u>set format</u>. There are <u>sections</u> that explain the <u>methods</u> used, the <u>information</u> that was found, and the writer's <u>conclusions</u> and <u>recommendations</u>.

3) Reports are <u>formal</u> documents — they're usually aimed at staff within the business who have <u>specialist knowledge</u> of the subject, so they often contain <u>complex data</u>.

Company *Newsletters* Keep Staff *Informed*

1) <u>Internal newsletters</u> are often a bit like <u>mini-newspapers</u> that report on events and developments within the business. They can be <u>formal</u> or <u>informal</u>, depending on the company.

2) Newsletters can be used to keep staff <u>informed</u> — this can help to <u>boost motivation</u> and <u>productivity</u> (see p38).

3) But they can also be <u>expensive</u> to produce — especially if paper copies are sent to <u>every</u> member of staff. And there's <u>no guarantee</u> that staff will read them, so they <u>shouldn't</u> be used to send <u>important</u> messages.

Newsletters can also be used to send information to <u>customers</u>.

GlassCo Gazette
Skylight sales go through the roof!

Employee does something clever/funny

Notices *are Put Up Where* All Employees *Can Read Them*

1) <u>Notices</u> are meant to be read by <u>the whole staff</u>, so they're put in places where all staff can see them.

2) They're often used for <u>publicising</u> events or changes to company policy.

3) Notices can be on <u>display</u> for a <u>long time</u>, giving all staff the chance to see them, possibly <u>many times</u>.

4) Notices are easy to <u>ignore</u> — some staff might <u>not see</u> them, so they're <u>no good</u> for <u>important</u> messages. And since they're displayed in <u>public</u>, they're also <u>not suitable</u> for <u>confidential</u> information.

Written communication — it has prose and cons...

The documents on this page all have their uses, but most modern firms <u>wouldn't</u> use them <u>all the time</u>. If you want to write a message to someone you work with, it's <u>quicker</u> and <u>easier</u> to send them an <u>email</u>.

More Written Communication

Businesses often send out written documents to their <u>customers</u> to keep them <u>informed</u> about their products. Sometimes, people <u>outside</u> the firm will send written messages (like CVs) <u>to</u> the business. Crazy.

Brochures, Leaflets <u>and Flyers</u> are Posted to Customers (mostly)

All these forms of written communication are types of <u>advertising</u>. Traditionally, they were all printed on <u>paper</u>, but it's now common to send flyers by <u>email</u> and make brochures available to <u>download</u> from the <u>internet</u>.

BROCHURES are like <u>glossy</u> magazines — they're used to <u>publicise new products</u> or give customers an <u>overview</u> of the existing product range.

CATALOGUES are similar, but they usually contain more information about <u>individual products</u>. This might include product <u>descriptions</u>, <u>prices</u>, and details of <u>how to order</u>.

FLYERS are usually <u>single-page</u> advertisements containing a <u>basic message</u> about a product or event. Flyers are often quite <u>visual</u> — pictures are used to make the page more <u>eye-catching</u>.

LEAFLETS usually contain a more <u>detailed message</u>.

CAR BOOT SALE
Sunday September 18th
Outside
The Old Sea Dog Pub
Admission: £2

Financial Documents <u>Need</u> to Be <u>Clear</u> and <u>Accurate</u>

1) Businesses must keep accurate records of all the <u>money</u> being spent and received. To do this, firms use a variety of <u>financial documents</u>.

Did I really spend this much on muesli?

2) One example is an <u>invoice</u> — this is a request for payment from a customer. Invoices include details of <u>who</u> the customer is, <u>what</u> they've bought, the <u>discount</u> they're entitled to, and <u>how much</u> they owe the firm.

INVOICE Incredibrek Ltd.	To:		Date of invoice: 6/2/2010 Payment due by: 6/4/2010		
Item	RRP	Disc. (%)	Unit Price	Qty	Total Price
Muesli 750 g	2.99	40	1.79	12	21.48
Muesli 2 kg	5.99	40	3.59	8	28.72
Muesli Ultra	11.99	25	8.99	10	89.90
Total payment due:					140.10

3) Financial documents must be <u>accurate</u> and <u>clear</u>. Invoices usually just contain addresses, product names, prices, and dates. The figures are often laid out in <u>columns</u> so that the details can be checked <u>quickly</u>.

4) A <u>financial report</u> might use <u>tables</u> and <u>charts</u> to help explain financial data.

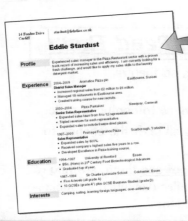

CVs are Used When Applying for a Job

1) A <u>curriculum vitae (CV)</u> is a summary of a person's <u>personal details</u>, <u>skills</u>, <u>qualifications</u>, <u>experience</u> and <u>interests</u>. Employers use them to assess <u>how suitable</u> someone is for a job.

2) CVs should be broken up into clear <u>sections</u> so that an employer can <u>find</u> the information they want <u>easily</u>.

3) A CV is designed to <u>impress</u> a potential employer, so good <u>spelling</u>, <u>punctuation</u> and <u>grammar</u> are important for making a <u>good first impression</u>.

That advert is pretty fly — but this one's flyer...

A few bits and pieces to think about on this page. All these written documents are usually printed on <u>paper</u> so that they're easy to <u>refer</u> to, but they can also be sent and received <u>electronically</u>. Grand.

Electronic Communication

Most of what you've seen so far in this section has been paper-based communication. But thanks to the magic of ICT, information can be exchanged <u>without using paper</u> at all. (Note: ICT is <u>not</u> magic. It's science.)

Paper Documents can be Sent by Fax

1) <u>Fax</u> machines send and receive <u>copies</u> of <u>paper documents</u> using a <u>telephone line</u>.

2) They're useful when the sender needs to make sure the receiver gets a document <u>quickly</u>. (Fax machines give you a 'receipt' to show that a document you've sent has been received.)

3) Faxes are <u>quick</u> and <u>cheap</u>, but not as quick or cheap as email (see below). Faxes can look a bit scruffy, so they're not ideal if presentation is important.

Faxes usually record the <u>date</u> and <u>time</u> they were sent.

> 05/10/2009   16:32   Lions Tours UK   Pg 1/1
>
> Mr Fox
> 56 Smithyard Close
> Millom
> LA18 7HG
>
> **Lions Tours**
> 7 Tour Lane
> Touringham
> TR3 7UG
> 01858 586300
> www.tourswirfenoar.co.uk
>
> Ref: Lion tour
> 12 November 2009
>
> Dear Mr Fox
>
> Thank you for expressing an interest in our fantastic Kenya

Email is Quick and Easy

<u>Email</u> is now the main way most firms send <u>written messages</u> quickly.

Advantages

1) Emails can be sent <u>all over the world</u> using the internet, or between a firm's staff over an <u>intranet</u>. It usually only takes <u>a few seconds</u> for an email to get from the sender to the receiver.

2) It's <u>easy</u> to send copies of the same email to <u>lots of people</u>, and <u>cheaper</u> than a phone call.

3) The receiver can either <u>print</u> the document themselves or just view it <u>on screen</u>, so <u>unnecessary paperwork</u> can be avoided.

4) Other <u>files</u> and <u>documents</u> can be <u>attached</u> to emails and sent at the same time.

Disadvantages

1) <u>Both</u> the sender and the receiver need access to a <u>computer</u> (or a suitable phone).

2) Emails are usually <u>less formal</u> than business letters — they're <u>not</u> usually well suited to <u>serious</u> messages like staff warnings.

3) They're also <u>not very confidential</u> — but some emails can be <u>encrypted</u> for extra security (see p26).

Look — this letter is on paper!
Haha! How quaint.

Internet Websites Can be Used to Exchange Information

Posting messages on a <u>website</u> can be a good way of making them available to the <u>general public</u>.

Advantages

1) <u>Anyone</u> with internet access can <u>view</u> the website. This means that messages can reach <u>large audiences</u> all over the world.

2) Some parts of a website can be <u>restricted</u> so that only <u>authorised users</u> with <u>passwords</u> can access them — this means businesses can <u>control</u> who is able to receive certain messages. E.g. a firm could post a <u>report</u> for <u>shareholders</u> without customers being able to read it.

3) Customers can also <u>send</u> messages and feedback to businesses through their websites. E.g. they might be able to <u>order products</u> online, or leave comments in a <u>guestbook</u>.

Disadvantages

1) People who <u>don't</u> have internet access may <u>miss out</u> on information (e.g. special offers).

2) It can be <u>difficult</u> to get people to look at your website.

Electronic communication leads to net gains...

Most modern businesses use <u>email</u> and the <u>internet</u> to send and exchange information. These media are <u>quick</u> and <u>convenient</u>, and they can reach a <u>large audience</u> without using three forests' worth of paper.

Electronic Communication

Email and websites aren't the only shows in town when it comes to electronic communication, of course. ICT creeps into <u>every corner</u> of the communication world, but it's not without its problems...

Mobile Phones _Can Send_ Text Messages _Using SMS_

1) <u>Mobile phones</u> can be used to send <u>SMS text messages</u> (<u>SMS</u> stands for <u>Short Message Service</u>). Single messages can be up to <u>160 characters</u> long (if you need to say more, you can <u>pay</u> for <u>extra texts</u>).

2) SMS messages are usually <u>cheaper</u> than a phone call.

3) But they're <u>fiddly</u> to type, and people often <u>abbreviate</u> words using textspeak. This makes them most useful for <u>short</u>, <u>informal</u> messages.

Electronic Notice Boards _Can be Regularly_ Updated

<u>Electronic notice boards</u> display information in the same way as a computer monitor.

Electronic notice boards are used a lot at <u>airports</u> and <u>railway stations</u> — to deliver messages to large groups of people.	The screen can cycle through <u>many pages</u> of information, displaying each one for a short time.	The information can be easily edited and displayed <u>straight away</u>. But they're <u>expensive</u>.	This page has been cancelled and replaced by a bus.

Loyalty Cards, RFID _Tags and Satnavs_ — All Very Clever

1) Many shops and supermarkets use <u>loyalty cards</u> to <u>collect data</u> about customers electronically.

2) Customers often collect <u>points</u> on their cards whenever they shop. These points can then be used to earn <u>money off</u> future purchases.

3) But the cards also <u>collect data</u> about the customers' shopping habits. This data can be used to produce a <u>profile</u> of each customer, so that they can be sent marketing materials that will <u>interest them</u>.

MARKETING TARGET ACQUIRED.

PROFILE: ENJOYS FRUIT, VEGETABLES, HANDBAGS ETC.

4) This <u>targeted marketing</u> is more <u>efficient</u> than sending out the same promotions to all customers.

<u>RFID</u> (Radio Frequency IDentification) tags can be recognised by a radio receiver. RFID tags can be attached to:
- <u>vehicles</u> — to automatically pay <u>tolls</u> for tunnels, bridges, and so on.
- <u>products</u> — so shops and delivery companies can <u>track</u> individual items.

This is an RFID tag. I'm actually tracking you right now.

<u>Satnavs</u> (Satellite navigation systems) also involve electronic communication.

1) A satnav system in a vehicle picks up signals from <u>satellites</u> orbiting the Earth. It uses these to calculate its <u>position</u> very <u>accurately</u>.

2) It can then use data stored in its <u>memory</u> to give <u>directions</u>.

Electronic Systems — _Good, but_ Not Cheap

Electronic <u>communication systems</u> are generally very <u>quick</u> and <u>efficient</u> if they're used the right way. But...

1) ICT equipment can be <u>expensive</u> to buy and maintain.

2) Staff may need <u>training</u> before they can use a system properly. This takes time and money.

ICT is useful, but not all systems go...

Remember, just because ICT systems are often expensive to buy, that doesn't mean they're not cheaper in the <u>long run</u>. Buying a computer and sending a million <u>emails</u> might be cheaper than buying a million <u>stamps</u>.

Face-to-Face Meetings

So, communication technology is amazing. I mean, seriously — wow. But sometimes it's <u>easier</u> and <u>more effective</u> to <u>meet</u> your fellow human beings in a single room for a chat. Scary stuff.

Face-to-Face Meetings Involve Oral Communication...

1) <u>Face-to-face meetings</u> involve a group of people getting together in the <u>same place</u> to discuss business.
2) <u>Informal</u> meetings can be like a conversation — without any <u>written record</u>.
3) <u>Formal</u> meetings are more carefully <u>organised</u> and <u>recorded</u>. They involve various <u>protocols</u> (see below).
4) In face-to-face meetings the <u>sender</u> (i.e. a person who says something) gets <u>instant feedback</u>. The sender can check that their message has been <u>understood</u> by asking questions (the listener can also ask questions to clarify anything they didn't understand).

...and Silent Communication

Humans communicate <u>silently</u> all the time — even if they <u>don't always realise</u> they're doing it.

1) <u>Body language</u> and <u>facial expressions</u> can be a giveaway (people can look bored, happy, angry...) Listeners may <u>interpret</u> a message in a particular way as a result of the speaker's body language.
2) <u>Touch</u> can also make a difference — e.g. people are sometimes judged on their <u>handshakes</u>.

Protocols are Rules Followed in Meetings

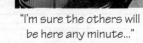
"I'm sure the others will be here any minute..."

Protocols are <u>rules</u> and <u>conventions</u> that people agree to stick to when communicating.

1) In <u>informal meetings</u>, protocols are often the same thing as <u>manners</u>. For example, it's often considered <u>rude</u> to <u>interrupt</u>, or <u>not listen</u> to others.
2) <u>Formal meetings</u> usually have many protocols. For example:

- The <u>agenda</u> outlines the topics that will be discussed. This should be sent to people in advance so that they can <u>plan</u> what they want to say.
- A <u>chairperson</u> controls the discussion — people may have to ask for <u>permission</u> to speak.
- <u>Minutes</u> are a <u>written record</u> of the topics discussed in the meeting.

Appraisals and AGMs are Face-to-Face Meetings

1) **APPRAISAL MEETINGS** — a <u>manager</u> and a <u>worker</u> discuss the worker's <u>performance</u> over the previous year. They then set <u>performance targets</u> for the worker for the next year.
2) Appraisal meetings are usually <u>private</u> and <u>face-to-face</u>. This makes it easier to raise <u>personal</u> issues and concerns.

1) **ANNUAL GENERAL MEETINGS (AGMs)** are held once a year by many large firms. The directors invite <u>all shareholders</u> to attend (see p4 for more about shareholders).
- The business provides a <u>report</u> on its performance to the shareholders.
- The <u>directors</u> can be <u>asked questions</u> about their performance by the shareholders.
2) AGMs are a good opportunity to <u>inform shareholders</u> of developments in the business.
3) They also allow the <u>directors</u> to get <u>feedback</u> from the owners of the business about their <u>performance</u>. Shareholders may be able to <u>vote</u> on the way the business is run.

Talk to the hand, 'cause the face ain't listening...

Meetings involve a lot of <u>talking</u> (or <u>oral communication</u>, if you prefer). Talking face to face with people can get quite <u>emotional</u>, especially if there's a <u>disagreement</u>. It's a lot more <u>personal</u> than all those letters.

Other Oral Communication

If Charles Dickens had wanted to communicate <u>orally</u> (i.e. using his voice) with somebody <u>far away</u>, he'd have had to shout. Thanks to telecommunication, shouting is now just something you can do for fun in libraries.

Telephones Allow Long-Distance Oral Communication

1) A <u>telephone</u> is a machine that converts... well... I guess you already know what a telephone is.

2) Telephone conversations allow <u>instant feedback</u>. But you <u>can't see body language</u>, which can make it <u>harder to interpret</u> the message.

3) <u>Mobile phones</u> allow people to be contacted even when they're not in the office. This is great for people who travel a lot as part of their job (as long as they can get a <u>signal</u>).

4) <u>Voicemail</u> can be used to <u>leave messages</u>. This means oral messages can be <u>delivered</u> at <u>any time</u> (though the sender won't get instant <u>feedback</u> this way).

5) Businesses often use <u>protocols</u> for telephone conversations (e.g. when they answer a call, staff usually give <u>their name</u> and the <u>company's name</u>).

Teleconferencing Links People in Different Places

<u>Teleconferencing</u> is when several people in <u>different locations</u> communicate as though they're in a <u>meeting</u> — usually using either <u>phone</u> or <u>internet</u> technology. There are <u>two main types</u> of teleconferencing.

> **AUDIO CONFERENCING** allows the people to communicate <u>orally</u>.
> - Each person has a <u>microphone</u> to talk into, and a <u>speaker</u> that outputs what other people are saying.
> - Audio conferences can be held using fairly basic telephones, so it's <u>not too expensive</u>.
> - On the downside, you <u>can't see</u> people's <u>body language</u>, so messages are easier to <u>misunderstand</u>.

> **VIDEO CONFERENCING** allows <u>oral</u> and <u>visual</u> communication.
> - It uses <u>speakers</u>, <u>microphones</u>, <u>video cameras</u> and <u>monitors</u> to transmit sound and images.
> - You can see people during the meeting, so it's more <u>human</u> and <u>personal</u>.
> - But the equipment is <u>more expensive</u> than normal telephones.

See p16 for more on teleconferencing.

Teleconferencing has become more popular in these globalised days. But it's <u>not</u> perfect.

1) There's always the risk of <u>technical failure</u> — if the machinery breaks down, then the meeting's <u>over</u>.

2) There can also be <u>delays</u> as messages are transmitted — this can make conversation <u>difficult</u>.

The Internet Can be Used to Transmit Oral Messages

The <u>internet</u> is used these days to carry all sorts of business communication.

1) <u>Webcasts</u> are a bit like normal **TV** broadcasts, except they're on the <u>internet</u>. E.g., companies that provide <u>training</u> often use webcasts.

2) <u>Podcasts</u> are <u>audio</u> or <u>video</u> files that people can download from a website and play on a computer or a portable device. Businesses use them to provide information about the company, or to promote new products. People who <u>subscribe</u> to podcasts automatically receive <u>updates</u>, so they can be a good way to keep people in touch with what your company is doing.

Survey question: Are you bored and frustrated in your job, and in life in general?

YES NO

3) <u>Webinars</u> are like presentations, but over the internet. They're held at <u>prearranged times</u>, and people who want to take part have to log on to a particular website. The audience can usually <u>participate</u> in webinars (e.g. by typing questions or comments for everyone else to see).

The telephone? Nope, doesn't ring any bells...

Telephones have been around since the nineteenth century — the flashy internet is a toddler by comparison. Learn about all the media on this page, then write down ten reasons why <u>webinar</u> is a <u>really stupid word</u>.

Visual Communication

A picture speaks a thousand words, apparently. If that's true, then a <u>logo</u> must speak maybe 500 or so. My point is that some forms of communication can say <u>a lot</u>, even if it doesn't <u>look</u> like they're saying a lot.

Names, Logos *and* Designs *Can Help Build a* Brand Image

1) Businesses try to give themselves <u>trading names</u> that are <u>unique</u>, <u>catchy</u> and <u>easy to remember</u>. They want you to think of <u>them</u> whenever you need a plumber/shampoo/bank/...

2) A <u>logo</u> is a <u>visual representation</u> of the business. It might include the <u>trading name</u> and some <u>visual images</u> summing up key messages about the business — to help it create an <u>identity</u>.

Some brands are so well known they can use a really <u>simple</u> logo (e.g. Nike's 'swoosh').

3) For example, a legal firm will probably want its logo to look neat, formal and professional (because this might make people think the firm is <u>professional</u> and <u>reliable</u> too — important for a legal firm).

Serious, sober, conventional. Just right.

4) Logos usually appear on <u>all</u> a business's written communications (letters, envelopes, brochures, adverts...), so it's important to get it <u>right</u>.

5) Even things like using the same <u>colour scheme</u> in all its communications can help a business create an identity — eventually customers might <u>connect</u> those colours with the business.

Advertisements *Promote Products And* Create an Image...

Adverts need to fit in with the <u>overall message</u> that a firm wants to communicate.

• Some adverts aim to communicate <u>specific information</u> about products and services.
• Some use images of <u>attractive people</u> to <u>link</u> the product to a <u>glamorous lifestyle</u>.
• Others can be plain <u>weird</u> — these aim to get people <u>thinking</u> and <u>talking</u> about the brand, even if no-one really understands what's going on.

It's good... but it's not quite us.

...*as do* Celebrity Endorsements *and* Slogans

1) **CELEBRITY ENDORSEMENTS**

• Large companies often ask famous people to <u>endorse</u> their products by appearing in advertising campaigns and smiling a bit.
• This can really <u>boost sales</u> — so a really popular celebrity can be paid <u>huge amounts</u> for their services.
• But if the celebrity gets involved in a scandal, it can make the firm look bad too.

Hi! I'm Bill Clinton. I'm famous, so you can trust my opinion about breakfast cereal.

CGP's strapline used to be: "Buy Our Books, Not Potatoes." To me, that just oozes wisdom.

2) **SLOGANS AND STRAPLINES**

• <u>Slogans</u> are phrases that are designed to be <u>catchy</u>. Sometimes they're even set to <u>music</u> (in which case they're called <u>jingles</u>).
• <u>Straplines</u> are captions that appear next to company <u>logos</u>.
• Both of these are a bit like a logo, only in <u>words</u> — they can help a firm project a certain image of itself, even though they're usually pretty short.

What a vain page — obsessed with image...

<u>Visual communication</u> (in logos, design, adverts etc.) can be a great way for businesses to reinforce the <u>image</u> they're trying to convey. And if they can rope in a <u>celeb</u> to say something nice, then all the better.

Revision Summary for Section Five

Well... that was hard work. Since I've gone to all the effort of making this section, the least you can do is answer some questions about it — you owe me. Plus, it'll be really useful revision for your exam.

But mainly, you owe me. Especially since I have to write the questions as well.

1) What's the purpose of communication, and what two groups of people are involved?

2) Give three methods of communication. Give an advantage of each.

3) List eight channels of communication.
Think up an example of a message that might be sent through each channel.

4) What is internal communication? Describe two benefits of good internal communication.

5) Give four examples of communication between a business and external stakeholders.

6) Describe three ways that poor external communication can cause problems for a business.

7) List eight barriers to communication. Give a quick explanation of each.

8) Explain four types of error that can be made in business documents.
Why is it important to check documents for errors before sending them?

9) List three situations when a business letter might be used to send a message.

10) Give three advantages and three disadvantages of business letters.

11) Describe these methods of internal written communication: memos, reports, newsletters, notices.
Give an advantage and a disadvantage of each.

12) What's the difference between a flyer and a brochure?

13) What's an invoice? Give four pieces of information that an invoice will contain.

14) What kind of information does a CV contain?

All right, you're halfway there. Give yourself a high five.
Okay — enough celebrating. The rest of these questions aren't going to answer themselves...

15) Are faxes quite good, or a bit rubbish? Discuss.

16) Give four reasons why email is great. Then give three problems with it — it's only fair.

17) How can a business restrict access to some parts of its website?

18) What does SMS stand for? What kind of message is SMS useful for?

19) Explain why supermarkets are so keen to give their customers loyalty cards.

20) What does RFID stand for? What can an RFID tag be used for?

21) Give two examples of how people can communicate silently in meetings.

22) Describe three protocols used in formal meetings.

23) Explain the purposes of appraisal meetings and AGMs.

24) What advantage does teleconferencing have over normal telephone calls?

25) Give an advantage and a disadvantage of video conferencing.

26) Describe the main features of webcasts, webinars and podcasts.

27) What's the purpose of a company logo? Why is it important to have a good logo?

28) What is a strapline?

How Businesses Use the Internet

The internet and the World Wide Web have changed the way firms communicate. Long gone are the days when communication was done during office hours only.

The Internet Creates All Sorts of Opportunities for Firms

1) The internet is basically a huge network of computers covering the whole world.

2) The World Wide Web (www) is a huge collection of websites that can be viewed by accessing the internet. To view these websites, you need a web browser.

3) Anyone can make a website — it can then be accessed by other computers elsewhere in the world, 24 hours a day.

4) Most modern businesses have their own website these days.

Good grief, Gerald — the internet is everywhere!
Gadzooks!

Websites Can Provide Customer Services...

The Internet is a really powerful tool for businesses. Used wisely, it can provide all sorts of customer services.

1) E-commerce (see next page) means buying and selling over the internet. Loads of firms these days let customers order goods online 24 hours a day. The goods can then either be posted to the customer or, for things like software and music, they can be downloaded straight away.

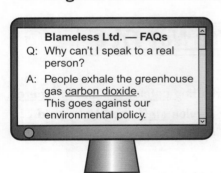
Blameless Ltd. — FAQs
Q: Why can't I speak to a real person?
A: People exhale the greenhouse gas carbon dioxide. This goes against our environmental policy.

2) Websites can also provide technical support. For example, a lot of software updates are provided over the internet.

3) Some companies let customers set up an online customer account. This allows customers to access services on the web (for example, bank websites let their customers pay bills online, mobile phone companies let customers top up their calling credit, and so on...).

4) Firms can also provide answers to frequently-asked questions (FAQs). This can be convenient for customers (since the information's available all the time). It also means the firm doesn't have to have employees answering the same questions over and over.

...and Give and Receive Information

The internet's also good for more general communication.

1) Websites can provide detailed information about products and services. It's cheaper for the firm than printing catalogues on paper.

2) Company websites can also give positive messages about what the firm does and how it does it. This might include the company's mission statement, or details of its social and environmental policies.

Read the heartwarming story of CGP's early years, for example.

Good communication goes both ways...

1) Customers can provide feedback via a firm's website. The firm can then react to this — maybe by answering questions, dealing with complaints or providing information that a customer's asked for.

2) Firms can also use feedback to make improvements to their products or customer service — firms often ask for opinions using online surveys.

3) And guestbooks allow customers to leave messages for the firm and other website visitors to read.

http://www.insertbadpunhere.com is not responding...

Websites have become a very important way for firms to communicate with their customers and other stakeholders. They can reach a wide audience, and messages can be exchanged quickly and easily. None of this information probably comes as a surprise, but make sure you know it, all the same.

Business Websites — Benefits and Costs

Buying and selling products and services online is called <u>e-commerce</u>.
Businesses need to think about the potential <u>costs</u> and <u>benefits</u> of e-commerce.

Websites Can be Used to Reach Wider Markets...

The internet provides extra <u>marketing</u> possibilities...

1) The internet can be accessed <u>all over the world</u> — this makes it possible to target potential customers in <u>foreign countries</u>.

2) A company can put marketing material on its <u>own</u> website, or <u>pay</u> to advertise on <u>other websites</u>.

3) Internet adverts can be <u>animated</u> and <u>interactive</u> — great for catching people's attention. And they usually contain a <u>direct link</u> to the company's own website.

...And Sell to These Markets 24/7

A good website can really help a firm's <u>competitiveness</u> and increase its <u>market share</u>.

1) Firms can <u>market</u> and <u>sell</u> goods through their websites 24 hours a day, 7 days a week (or '<u>24/7</u>').

2) 24/7 marketing and selling can give e-commerce firms an <u>advantage</u> over traditional 9 to 5 businesses. Customers shop <u>from home</u> at a time that's convenient <u>for them</u>.

Websites Can Reduce Costs — But They're Not Free

E-commerce can <u>reduce costs</u> in lots of ways. For example...

1) Putting product information online saves the cost of printing and distributing <u>catalogues</u> and <u>brochures</u>.

2) Online customer services (e.g. FAQs) may mean that fewer customer service <u>staff</u> need to be paid.

3) Businesses that only <u>sell</u> online rather than in High Street <u>shops</u> save money on <u>rent</u>.

But for some businesses, the <u>costs</u> of the website could be <u>greater</u> than the savings.

1) <u>Setting up</u> a website costs money. Firms often need the help of <u>specialist website designers</u>. And things like <u>online payment facilities</u> can be expensive to set up.

2) Once the website is up and running, staff will be needed to <u>maintain</u> and <u>update</u> it.

3) The internet is always available, so staff may need to work <u>outside normal office hours</u> to maintain it or offer <u>customer support</u>. These staff will need to be <u>paid</u> for their extra time.

Websites Can Give Businesses More to Worry About

1) E-commerce firms collect <u>confidential data</u> from their customers (e.g. phone numbers, credit card details).

2) Firms need to protect this information from <u>unauthorised users</u> by making their websites <u>secure</u>. Customers who have money and information stolen may never come back — or may even <u>sue</u>. This could easily lead to the firm getting a <u>bad reputation</u>.

3) The internet can help a firm reach <u>wider markets</u>. But it also means that competitors from <u>all over the world</u> can compete in the firm's 'home' market.

We may look harmless, but try to steal our data and we'll destroy you.

Yeah! Tell 'em, boss!

There's no point being short-sited...

For most <u>large</u> businesses, having a website is <u>essential</u> to compete in the market. But for some more traditional firms, a website may <u>not</u> be what their customers <u>want</u> — the costs could <u>outweigh</u> the benefits.

Websites and the Law

There are <u>laws</u> even in <u>cyberspace</u>. It's hard for the law to keep up with <u>cybercrime</u>, though. This isn't a very exciting page — there's no such thing as a cyber-car-chase.

Personal Data Collected on Websites Must be Protected

Not surprisingly, your old pal the <u>Data Protection Act 1998</u> (see p27) applies to <u>websites</u>.

1) All UK-based websites that collect <u>personal data</u> from visitors have to obey the Act.

2) This includes protecting private information like <u>email addresses</u>, <u>usernames</u> and <u>passwords</u>.

3) E-commerce sites that collect <u>financial data</u> and customer <u>addresses</u> need to be especially careful — this means investing in good online <u>security</u>.

Websites Can't Copy Material Without Permission...

Websites are also subject to the <u>Copyright, Designs and Patents Act 1989</u>.

1) This Act means it's illegal to <u>copy</u> text, data or images, without <u>permission</u> from the copyright holder.

2) So businesses need to be <u>careful</u> about what they put on their website — if they want to use somebody else's material, they have to <u>ask permission</u> and they may have to <u>pay a fee</u>.

3) Website owners breaking this law could face an <u>unlimited fine</u> — especially if they've <u>profited</u> from it.

...Must Sell Products Legally...

1) Websites selling goods and services have to follow the <u>same laws</u> as High Street shops, including the <u>Supply of Goods and Services Act (1982)</u> and the <u>Sale and Supply of Goods Act (1994)</u>.

2) These laws state that <u>every</u> product (including products sold <u>online</u>) must:

   i) be <u>fit for its purpose</u> — i.e. it should <u>do the job</u> it's designed for.

   ii) <u>match its description</u> — so all online product information must be <u>accurate</u>.

   iii) be of <u>satisfactory quality</u> — it should <u>last</u> a reasonably long time, and not have <u>other faults</u> that cause problems for the buyer (e.g. a fridge that buzzes loudly).

3) If products don't come up to scratch, customers are legally entitled to an <u>exchange</u> or a <u>replacement</u>. For <u>e-commerce</u> businesses, this can be <u>expensive</u> — they may also have to pay the costs of <u>postage</u>.

4) Businesses must also do all they can to make sure their websites are <u>accessible</u> to people with <u>disabilities</u>.

...And Follow Distance-Selling Laws

1) <u>Distance selling</u> means selling where there is <u>no face-to-face contact</u> between buyer and seller.

2) The <u>Consumer Protection (Distance Selling) Regulations 2000</u> give customers three main rights:

   i) Websites must provide <u>clear information</u> about the firm and its products <u>before</u> customers buy.

   ii) They must give customers <u>written confirmation</u> of any orders placed — usually by <u>email</u>.

   iii) Customers have a seven-day <u>cooling-off period</u> when they can <u>cancel</u> the order without penalty.

3) Firms should always use an <u>encrypted</u> part of their website to collect payment.

An encrypted web page has "https://", rather than just "http://" in the address — the 's' stands for 'secure'.

4) As usual, businesses that break these rules can be <u>fined</u>. Serious fraud can lead to prison sentences.

My pizza arrived late — there was a cooling-off period...

They may be online, but e-commerce businesses deal with <u>real people</u>, <u>real money</u> and <u>personal information</u>. It can cost money to obey the laws, but breaking them can lead to <u>fines</u> and damage the firm's <u>reputation</u>.

Success of Business Websites

Businesses need to know how <u>successful</u> their websites are to make sure they're <u>worth</u> the investment. There's no point splashing out cash on a fancy website that doesn't achieve anything except look pretty.

Firms Need to Measure the Success of their Websites

There are different ways for a firm to do this. For instance, they can measure:
- how many '<u>hits</u>' they get — i.e. how many times the page is viewed,
- <u>how long</u> people look at their website for,
- how many <u>repeat visitors</u> they get.

A firm can even track <u>where</u> people linked to their site <u>from</u> (so if the firm placed an advert on another website, it can see how successful it was).

This is all very nice, but what a company is <u>really</u> interested in is whether their website has helped to:

1. Increase Brand Awareness

1) A firm's website is a good place to tell potential customers about their <u>brand</u> (see p6).
2) <u>Brand awareness</u> can be measured by <u>surveys</u> (often online) that ask people where they <u>heard about</u> various different businesses.

2. Increase Overall Sales and Market Share

1) It's easy to track how many sales are made <u>online</u> — if these are increasing, then that's a good sign. But customers may just be buying through the firm's website <u>instead</u> of through shops or mail-order.
2) So a good website (like any other promotion) will ideally increase a firm's <u>overall sales</u>.
3) A successful website should help a firm increase its <u>market share</u> (market share is the <u>percentage</u> of all <u>sales</u> in the market that a firm receives — see p5).

3. Reduce Costs

1) A firm might be able to <u>reduce</u> the number of <u>stores</u> it operates if online business really takes off.
2) If online <u>customer support</u> is effective, there should be <u>fewer calls</u> to the company's telephone helpline.
3) Online product information should lead to <u>less demand</u> for <u>paper</u> catalogues and brochures.

But remember that none of these measures is <u>totally</u> reliable in measuring the website's success. <u>Other factors</u> might also be affecting these measures (e.g. sales might be increasing because of other <u>marketing campaigns</u>, or because <u>customer habits</u> have changed).

Websites Won't be Vital For All Businesses

It was a lot easier when we just went to the grocer's.

ADD TO BASKET?

1) Websites don't allow <u>face-to-face</u> contact. Some firms might decide a website wouldn't really help them (e.g. if they make a point of providing <u>personal</u> advice in a traditional way).
2) Some businesses will feel they need to have a website as part of their general marketing 'presence' — it's what customers expect. They may choose just to have a <u>basic</u>, <u>inexpensive</u> website that provides information and <u>contact details</u>, but not worry too much about anything fancy.

Successful website — top of the hit parade...

Most businesses now have a website of some sort, but some firms will benefit <u>much more</u> than others. If a website isn't earning its keep, it may need to be <u>redesigned</u> and <u>relaunched</u>.

Creating a Website

So you now know everything about websites. Congratulations. Oh... hang on... one last thing...
You also need to know a few things to consider when actually making a website.

Plan the Website Around the Budget, Content and Users

Budget

1) The more ambitious the website, the bigger the budget a firm will need. Or to put it another way, if you don't have a big budget, keep your ambitions realistic. A really fancy website might have loads of interactive content and look really professional. But it all costs.

2) Secure e-commerce facilities also cost — so firms with a small budget need to work out whether they're likely to earn the money back through internet sales.

Content

1) Think about the purpose of the website — this will decide the content.

2) You might be able to provide information using mainly simple text and diagrams. But if you want to thrill or entertain, you might go for videos and interactive content — this is more complex, more expensive and takes up more memory.

Users and their equipment

The site's content needs to meet the needs of the people who'll be using it.

1) For example, children will prefer sites that have plenty of bright colours, games and animations.

2) Sites designed for adults (e.g. news sites) will probably be very different in tone.

3) You also need to think about the different equipment people might be using...

- The speed of internet connections varies from place to place. Website designers need to make sure that most users will be able to download content at a reasonable speed. If a website runs too slowly, many users will get tired of waiting and go elsewhere.

- There are also many different internet browsers available — the site should be compatible with as many as possible. If it's not, some users won't be able to use the site.

Develop, Test and Roll Out the Website

TECHNICAL DEVELOPMENT

1) Once the planning's done, the website needs to be constructed.

2) This can be done using specialist web-authoring software (see p77). Web designers may be employed to set up the website — depending on how complex the design is.

3) When the development is finished, it needs to be tested for bugs and other problems. This should include testing on different browsers, internet connections and hardware. This helps to make sure that all users will be able to get good access to the site.

ROLL-OUT AND MAINTENANCE

1) Businesses roll out their websites by uploading them to an internet server.

2) Sometimes complex websites are rolled out one section at a time — e.g. a few initial bits may be published first, and links added to it once any technical glitches have been ironed out.

3) Once the site is up and running, it needs to be maintained. Content needs to be kept up to date, and links to other websites need to be checked to make sure they still work.

Charlotte's Web was never this complicated...

Making a website is a creative process, but web designers should keep all the factors on this page in mind. Different businesses will need different things from their sites, but all websites should serve a purpose.

Revision Summary for Section Six

Turns out there's a lot to say about websites. There's the business side about all the costs and benefits, and then there's all the technical development stuff too. I don't know about you, but I really fancy some revision questions to refresh my memory.

1) What is the World Wide Web, and what kind of software do you need to view it?

2) Give four types of customer service that can be provided on a website.

3) Describe two types of information that a firm might put on its website.

4) What is e-commerce?

5) What is 24/7 marketing, and why might it help firms with a website become more competitive?

6) List three ways that a website can reduce business costs, and three ways it could increase them.

7) How can a website cause problems for a business?

8) List five types of personal data that a firm might collect on its website.

9) Explain how the Copyright, Designs and Patents Act 1989 affects website owners.

10) a) Give three criteria that all products sold on websites have to meet by UK law.
    b) What are customers entitled to if products don't meet these criteria?

11) What three rights do website customers have under 'Distance Selling law'?

12) Why might increasing sales on a website not mean that sales are increasing overall?

13) Give three ways that a firm might try to measure the success of its website.

14) Explain three factors that businesses should consider when planning their websites.

15) Describe the different stages of developing a website.

16) What is meant by rolling out a website?

17) Give two things that need to be done during website maintenance.

Software Applications

This last Section is all about <u>using software</u> to make different types of <u>business documents</u>. It's all about getting ready for your <u>computer-based assessment</u>.

You'll Need to Practise Practise Practise

Now then... learning how to use a piece of software <u>isn't</u> the kind of thing that's best done <u>just</u> by reading a book. You <u>really</u> need to:

- sit yourself down <u>in front of a computer</u>,
- find out how to use <u>all</u> the different features mentioned on these pages — using the software you'll be using for your computer-based assessment.

Not like this.

We <u>don't know</u> exactly what software you'll be using on your exam day — so we can't tell you in this book <u>exactly what buttons</u> to press to use all the different features (even different versions of the <u>same</u> piece of software can look very different).

Like this — look how much fun computers can be.

BUT...   We've got some animated computer-based <u>tutorials</u> that will <u>talk you through</u> how to use some of the <u>trickier features</u> for some <u>common pieces of software</u>.

Have a look at the <u>inside front cover</u> of this book for where to find them.

Okay, now it's on with the show...

Open, Save and Print Using The File Menu

You'll probably need the <u>File menu</u> several times in your exam — it's similar in most pieces of software. You can use it to <u>Save</u>, <u>Print</u> and <u>Open</u> documents.

- Click on the <u>File</u> menu, then...

① ...to Open a document:
- Click on <u>Open...</u>,
- Find your document and click on it,
- Click on the button marked <u>Open</u>.

② ...to save a document with a different name:
- Click on <u>Save As...</u>,
- Type the <u>name</u> you want to give to your document in the <u>File Name</u> box,
- Click on the button marked <u>Save</u>.

③ ...to print a document:
- Click on <u>Print...</u>

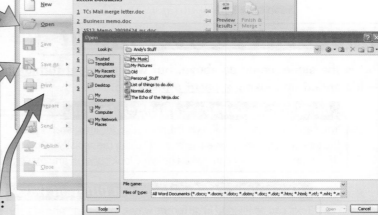

You might know quicker ways to do this stuff. If so, that's fine — do it the way you like best. But if in doubt, always head for the <u>File menu</u>.

Somebody save me — I don't care how you do it...

I know, I know... maybe you know how to do all this stuff already. But don't get all <u>complacent</u> on me — you could easily <u>lose marks</u> in the exam if you save over a file you still need, or print in the wrong format. And if you're <u>not</u> confident about this stuff, try to find yourself a computer and <u>practise</u>. Save a file as Dave. Then close it, open it again and print it. Then save another copy of the file as Emma. Repeat until happy.

Word Processors: Text Formatting

Word processors are designed specifically for editing text (words) — ideal for documents such as memos (p41). Word processors let you format text (change its appearance) in plenty of ways, but remember that no amount of prettiness will cover up for poor spelling, punctuation and grammar.

Formatting Can Make Text Attractive and Readable...

Memos are usually used for internal communication (see p38). They're not too fancy — they just contain the names of the sender and receivers, the date, the subject, and the message itself.

Basically the same information as at the start of an email.

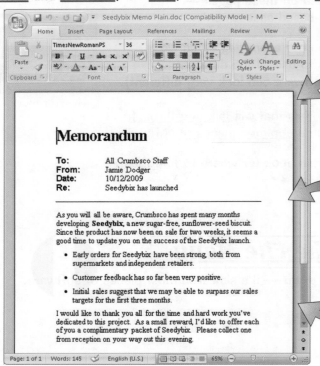

You can Change the Size of Text

- The font size of normal text is often between 10 and 12 points. Most people find that fairly easy to read.
- Headings are often printed in a larger size of text.

Fonts can be Formal or Informal

Word processors let you choose from various fonts. You should choose a font that's appropriate for the type of document, and the document's audience.

Formal business documents usually use neat, clear fonts. Most of this memo is in Times New Roman, but there's a bit of Arial in there at the top, too.

For informal documents, other fonts might be more **eye-catching**.

Bullet Points Draw People's Attention

- You can indent text so that the line starts further away from the margin.
- And bullet points can draw people's attention to things that are important.

...But Don't Go Crazy With It

This is the same memo as above, but with different formatting — it's ended up looking a bit of a mess.

Highlighting can Draw Attention to Text

You can highlight text using **bold**, *italics*, underlining and colour. It's best not to use these too much though (especially in formal documents) — they can make the page look childish and messy.

Paragraphs can be Aligned in Different Ways

Text can be aligned in different ways. Left-align and justify are the most common for normal text. This version of the memo uses a range, including centre- and right-alignment.

You can also adjust the line spacing of text. Increasing the space between lines can make text less crowded and easier to read.

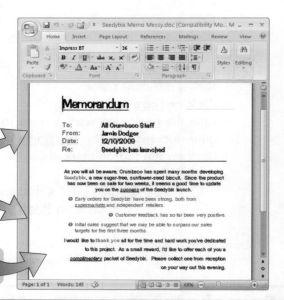

Underlining text — it's the highlight of my day...

You should be able to use all the techniques on this page, but don't throw them all in just because you can — keep the tone of your message in mind. In the exam, you might have to explain your formatting choices. If you're struggling to work out how to do any of these things, try clicking the right mouse button.

Word Processors: Text and Graphics

Sometimes a business will want to produce a document that contains more than just text.
Luckily, word processors can handle <u>graphics</u>, too — you can use them to <u>combine</u> text and pictures.

Text Boxes and Clip Art Can Make a Page Attractive

Some business documents use a mixture of <u>written</u> and <u>visual</u> communication.
<u>Flyers</u> (p42) often combine text and graphics to make a big impact. Here's an example.

Text Boxes can be Dragged Around

<u>Text boxes</u> let you keep chunks of text <u>separate</u> from the main text on the page. You can give them <u>borders</u> and <u>shading</u> (like the heading on this page).

Clip Art is Ready-Made Pictures

Word processors often have their own collections of <u>clip art</u> (ready-made pictures) that you can <u>insert</u> into your documents.

You can Wrap Text in Different Ways

<u>Text wrap</u> lets you position text <u>around</u> objects in various ways (see below). You can also usually <u>customise</u> how the text wraps by dragging the '<u>wrap points</u>' (like the ones around the spanner).

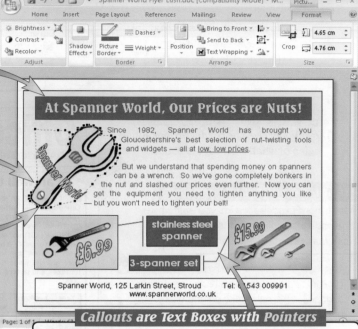

Callouts are Text Boxes with Pointers

Callouts are useful for <u>labelling</u> things and making speech bubbles. You can usually change the <u>direction</u> of the pointer.

You Can Also Put Graphics in the Background

<u>Advertisements</u> often aim for <u>visual impact</u> as well — not loads of information.

Spanner World has included its <u>logo</u> and its <u>website address</u> on its flyer <u>and</u> its advert.

You can Overlay Text on Graphics

Putting text <u>on top</u> of a graphic is a really useful technique — it can make <u>visual</u> documents like adverts look a lot more interesting.

WordArt Makes Text Look Pretty

You can use WordArt to bend text into <u>shapes</u>, give it <u>shading</u>, and add <u>borders</u> to the letters.

Borders can help things to Stand Out

You can put <u>borders</u> around most objects in a word processor, including the <u>page</u> itself. You can change the <u>style</u>, <u>thickness</u> and <u>colour</u> of borders.

Contains scenes of a graphic textual nature...

Word processors are really useful for making <u>basic</u> flyers, leaflets, etc. But most firms would probably make their documents using specialist <u>graphics packages</u> — so they look a bit more snazzy and professional.

Word Processors: Text and Graphics

You need to be able to present data in an <u>appropriate</u> way — and that could well mean <u>tables</u> and <u>charts</u>. Make sure you can create all the effects in the newsletter below.

Newsletters Can Include Columns, Tables and Diagrams

<u>Newsletters</u> are often a bit like mini newspapers, with text laid out in columns. They may also include data in the form of <u>charts</u>, <u>graphs</u> and <u>diagrams</u>. Your word processor should be able to handle all this stuff.

This newsletter has a colourful and eye-catching <u>banner</u>. (<u>WordArt</u> is good for this.)

<u>Large</u>, <u>bold</u> headlines to <u>draw attention</u>. They should give the reader an <u>instant idea</u> of what the story is about.

Text Can be Split into Columns

Most word processors let you split the page into <u>columns</u> of text. This can make the text easier to read.

The text in the columns has been <u>justified</u> (the left- and right-hand edges are both aligned). This can make columns look <u>tidy</u>, but watch out for <u>big gaps</u> between words.

Tables are Good For Presenting Data Clearly

Word processors usually have a tool for making tables. You can change the number of <u>rows</u> and <u>columns</u> and tinker with the <u>format</u> till your table looks <u>gorgeous</u>.

You can also <u>import</u> tables from other places (see below), which can make life easier.

<u>Graphs</u> and <u>charts</u> can be a good way to represent data <u>visually</u>. Here, it's much easier to see the change on the graph than it is from the numbers in the table.

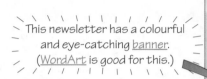

OfficeShed News
Issue 35
Jan 2010
The monthly newsletter for OfficeShed Employees

Farewell to the Fax Machine

It's the end of an era for OfficeShed — after 25 years of selling fax machines, we've decided that there's just not enough demand to justify keeping them in stock any longer. Here are the sales figures for faxes and laptops since 2000:

Year	Laptop sales	Fax sales
2000	1236	954
2001	1470	920
	1510	765
	2013	590
2004	2465	424
2005	2953	311
2006	3730	230
2007	5005	157
2008	5660	92
2009	5840	66

As you can see, fax sales have dropped dramatically in the last ten years as more up-to-date electronic devices have taken over. Laptops have become some of our biggest-selling items, and have been boosted in recent years by the introduction of netbooks. Combined with email and efaxes, there's just no way the old-style fax machine can compete, so we've decided that the time has come to pull the plug on our paper-printing pal. We'll sell through our existing stock before discontinuing the range, so if you'd like to grab one, it could be now or never.
Derek Jacks, Sales Manager

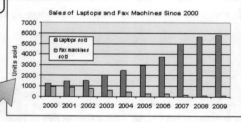

Sales of Laptops and Fax Machines Since 2000

OfficeShed Loft Insulation Will Leave Competitors Lagging

OfficeShed has supplied stationery and other office equipment to its customers since 1977. But now we have exciting plans to expand our range of products into energy-saving office solutions, including loft insulation.

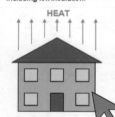

HEAT

As the diagram clearly shows, hot air rises, so heat escapes rapidly through roofs that don't have insulation. Businesses can make massive savings on their energy bills simply by investing in the right materials, and we intend to target new and existing customers who we believe could benefit from this product.
More news on our marketing strategy for this in the next issue.
Lisa Kitt, Marketing Director

Page: 1 of 1 | Words: 276 | English (U.S.) | 74%

Charts and Graphs Can be Imported

Sometimes it's possible to use a diagram from <u>another program</u> (like a <u>spreadsheet</u> or a <u>database</u>) in a word processor document. (This graph was made in a spreadsheet, for example — see p65.)

Word Processors Often Have Simple Drawing Tools

Word processors often have some basic <u>drawing</u> tools — for example, you might be able to draw <u>simple shapes</u> like rectangles, triangles, arrows and so on. This house was made out of simple shapes (which were then <u>grouped</u> together).

Inserting graphics — it's a matter of great import...

For a change, I thought I'd lay out the text in this box in columns. | But it's not really <u>appropriate</u> here. It's best not to do fancy things | just because you can — leave it for times when it'll actually <u>help</u>.

Word Processors: Business Letters

A <u>template</u> is a standard document containing <u>pre-set</u> formats and layouts. Word processors usually come with a set of <u>ready-made</u> templates. But you can make your own from a document you've already made.

Business Letters _Usually Follow a_ Standard Format

Businesses send <u>different types</u> of letters to different stakeholders (p4), but the formatting often doesn't change much. Here's an example of a letter responding to a <u>job application</u>.

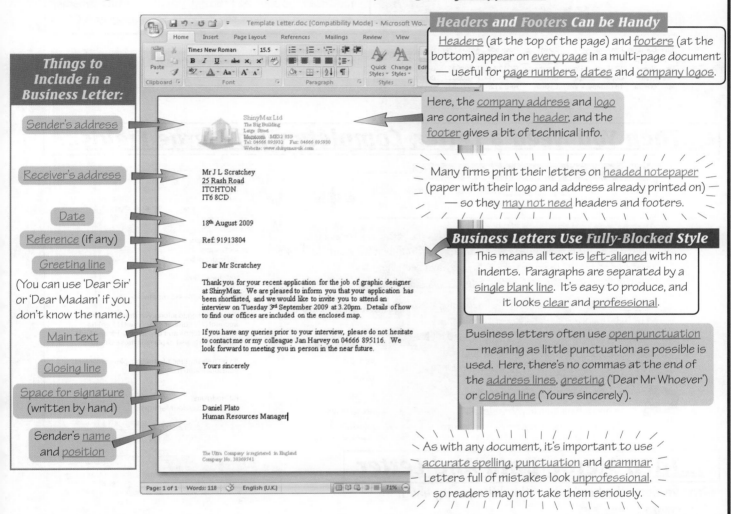

Things to Include in a Business Letter:

- <u>Sender's address</u>
- <u>Receiver's address</u>
- <u>Date</u>
- <u>Reference</u> (if any)
- <u>Greeting line</u>
  (You can use 'Dear Sir' or 'Dear Madam' if you don't know the name.)
- <u>Main text</u>
- <u>Closing line</u>
- <u>Space for signature</u> (written by hand)
- Sender's <u>name</u> and <u>position</u>

Headers and Footers Can be Handy

<u>Headers</u> (at the top of the page) and <u>footers</u> (at the bottom) appear on <u>every page</u> in a multi-page document — useful for <u>page numbers</u>, <u>dates</u> and <u>company logos</u>.

Here, the <u>company address</u> and <u>logo</u> are contained in the <u>header</u>, and the <u>footer</u> gives a bit of technical info.

Many firms print their letters on <u>headed notepaper</u> (paper with their logo and address already printed on) — so they <u>may not need</u> headers and footers.

Business Letters Use Fully-Blocked Style

This means all text is <u>left-aligned</u> with no indents. Paragraphs are separated by a <u>single blank line</u>. It's easy to produce, and it looks <u>clear</u> and <u>professional</u>.

Business letters often use <u>open punctuation</u> — meaning as little punctuation as possible is used. Here, there's no commas at the end of the <u>address lines</u>, <u>greeting</u> ('Dear Mr Whoever') or <u>closing line</u> ('Yours sincerely').

As with any document, it's important to use <u>accurate spelling</u>, <u>punctuation</u> and <u>grammar</u>. Letters full of mistakes look <u>unprofessional</u>, so readers may not take them seriously.

Letters _and_ Other Documents _Can be Used as_ Templates

1) Once you've produced a letter you're happy with, you can save it as a <u>template</u>. Templates are 'starting points' for other documents. Templates allow a business to <u>quickly</u> produce letters with the right <u>style</u> and <u>formatting</u> without starting from scratch every time.

2) Some details (names, addresses etc.) will need to <u>change</u> for each receiver. This can be done <u>manually</u>, or by using <u>mail-merge</u> fields in the letter (see the next page).

3) You can set up templates for <u>other types</u> of document, too — e.g. memos, notices, agendas...

4) Word processors usually come with <u>built in</u> templates. These are often a good <u>starting point</u> for documents — they give you the <u>basic layout</u>, and you can change the <u>details</u> to suit your needs.

Better template than never...

Many businesses produce a lot of <u>very similar documents</u> (especially <u>letters</u>), day in, day out. Templates can <u>save time</u>, but make sure you know how to lay out a business letter <u>from scratch</u> too — examiners love it.

Word Processors: Mail Merge

Mail merge lets you <u>merge</u> data from a <u>data source</u> (e.g. spreadsheet or database) into a word processor document. This is <u>incredibly</u> useful when you need to send out stacks and stacks of <u>standard letters</u> with just a few details (like the name and address) changed each time.

First, You'll Need Some Data to Merge...

Organise Your Data

You'll need the source of the <u>data</u> that you want to merge into your letter. Here, the data's in a <u>spreadsheet</u> (p62).

The first row shows the names of the <u>data fields</u>.
Other rows each contain one complete <u>record</u> (see p68).

...Then You Need a Letter, Complete with Merge Fields...

Write the Letter and Add the Fields

Here's the <u>standard letter</u> that needs to go to all the customers whose details are in the above spreadsheet.

But there are some details missing that will be <u>different</u> for each customer — the name, address and account number, for example. Instead of filling these details in, <u>fields</u> have been inserted — these are the things inside <<<u>double angled brackets</u>>>.

<u>Inserting</u> the field names can be a bit fiddly, and usually involves a few different menus — like this, for example. But the <u>basic idea</u> is <u>always the same</u> — you're creating <u>links</u> from your letter to a field in your data source.

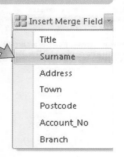

The animated tutorial will talk you through all this in more detail. See the inside front cover for more info.

...Then Merge Data And Letter

You've done the hard bit — this bit's pretty easy.

Merge the Data

It's pretty straightforward to <u>merge</u> the data and <u>print</u> your letters. But you should <u>preview</u> your letters first — just to make sure all's well.

When you preview the letters, the <u>field names</u> are replaced by data from <u>one record</u> in your data source. You can flick through all the letters (i.e. use data from each record in turn) to check they're all okay.

<u>Check</u> your letters carefully <u>before</u> you print them.

If you're happy that all the different letters look okay, you can <u>finish</u> the mail merge and print the letters (or email them).

You can even edit the individual letters if they need to be customised somehow.

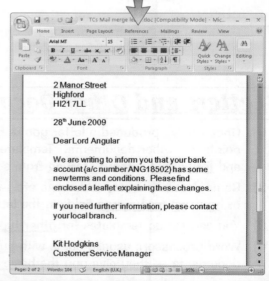

Congratulations, <<Title>> <<Surname>>! You've won!

Mail merge looks more fiddly than it actually is — the key is <u>practice</u>. So on your birthday, why not use mail merge to write standard thank-you letters to all your friends and relatives. They'll be <u>so</u> impressed.

Revision Summary for Section Seven

There's lots you need to know about word processing. And you don't just need to know about word processors and business documents so that you can answer questions about them (this is important, mind). You also need to be able to <u>do</u> things on a word processor. That means there are a few practical questions in the list below — you should definitely have a go at these as well. As always, if you find you're not sure about something, then make sure you do something about it — otherwise you're just storing up problems for yourself come Exam day.

1)   Which menu contains the options for opening, printing and saving files?

2)   What are memos used for in a business?

3)   What information would you expect to see at the top of a memo?

4)   Describe five different types of text formatting. Suggest a situation where each one might be used.

5)   What problem can using too much formatting create (especially in a formal business document)?

6)   Describe one technique often used on flyers to make a visual impact.

7)   What is clip art?

8)   What is meant by text-wrapping?

9)   What are callouts?

10) How do you change the look of a text box's border on <u>your</u> word-processing software?

11) Use a word processor to create a flyer for a shop that sells fruit and vegetables.
     Use text boxes, clip art, WordArt and borders, and overlay some text on a graphic.

12) In the world of word processing, what does it mean if text is 'justified'?

13) What does 'importing' a picture mean?

14) Business letters use 'fully-blocked style' and 'open punctuation'. What do these terms mean?

15) What is meant by a template? How can templates save businesses time?

16) Use a word processor template to write a short business letter confirming a customer order.
     Include a (made-up) name and address for the person you're writing to.
     Save your letter in a place where you'll be able to find it again.

17) Why might a business want to use mail merge?

18) What is a mail-merge field?

19) Why should you preview mail-merged letters before you print them out?

20) a) Make a spreadsheet containing three (made-up) names and addresses.
       You should include the following fields: Title (Mr, Mrs, Miss, etc.), First name, Family name
                                                   House number, Street, Town, Postcode
    b) Open your letter from Q16. Insert mail-merge fields where the name and address currently are.
    c) Use your word processor's mail-merge facility to produce three letters, one to each
       of your made-up people from part a).

Spreadsheets

Spreadsheets are big grids full of fun. Assuming that your idea of fun is entering data (numbers or text), performing calculations, and producing charts and graphs, of course.

Spreadsheets Contain Rows and Columns of Cells

Each of the little boxes on a spreadsheet is called a cell.

Cells Belong to Rows and Columns

Cell references tell you which column and row a cell is in. For example, the cell in column A, row 2 has cell reference A2.

- To enter data, just click on a cell and start typing.
- To edit a cell's contents, click in the formula bar above the grid. (Double clicking on a cell sometimes works too).

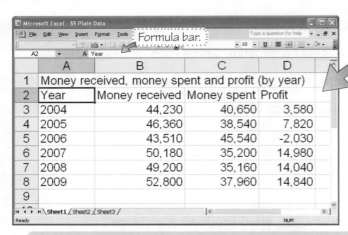

Formula bar.

Use Titles and Headings

Spreadsheets should have a title in the first row to explain what the data shows. Each row and column should also be labelled. Each row or column of data is called a data series.

You can also put titles and other info into headers and footers (see p59). These only show up when you print.

You Can Change the Sizes of Cells

You can adjust the heights of rows and the widths of columns until your data fits neatly into the cells.

Validation rules control what data can be put into a cell, e.g. only text, or only numbers between 1 and 100, and so on.

Formatting Makes Spreadsheets Clearer and Prettier

Here's the same data, but with an extra column added, and some more formatting applied.

Text Can be Formatted as Usual

Data in cells can be formatted like in a word processor — e.g. you can make it bold, underlined and italic, and align it to the left, right or centre.

Cells Can Be Merged and Added

Here, cells B1, C1, D1 and E1 have been merged — they've become a single cell.
Column A has also been inserted to add some extra information. The cells have been merged, and the text has been rotated to fit the space.

Borders Help to Split Data Up

Borders help to keep sections of a spreadsheet separate. You can choose the thickness, style and colour of borders.

	A	B	C	D	E
1		Money received, money spent and profit (by year)			
2		Year	Money received	Money spent	Profit
3		2004	£44,230	£40,650	£3,580
4		2005	£46,360	£38,540	£7,820
5		2006	£43,510	£45,540	-£2,030
6		2007	£50,180	£35,200	£14,98
7		2008	£49,200	£35,160	£14,040
8		2009	£52,800	£37,960	£14,840

(Financial years ending 31st March)

This sheet uses a coloured fill for titles and headings, but the cells containing data are left plain white.

Add a Splash of Colour

You can change the fill colour of cells, and the font colour within cells. This can make it easier to pick out particular types of data (and make the sheet look nicer).

You can use conditional formatting to set some colours to come up automatically — e.g. negative numbers can be highlighted in red.

Put Data in a cell? Why, what's he done, Worf?

Spreadsheets are a good way to organise data series (especially numerical data) into rows and columns. Formatting can help to make spreadsheets easier to read — as always, you're aiming for clarity.

Spreadsheets: Using Formulas

Spreadsheets are really useful for dealing with <u>numbers</u> — each cell can perform <u>calculations</u>.
So using a spreadsheet is like having about a <u>tonne</u> of calculators on your desk.

Formulas Are Used for Calculations

The animated tutorial will take you through all this step by step.

	A	B	C	D
	Product name	Number sold	Selling price	Money made from sales
1				
2	Yellow T-shirt	6,753	£6.99	=B2*C2
3	Blue T-shirt	8,115	£6.99	
4	Black T-shirt	11,654	£6.99	
5	Denim shorts	3,420	£9.99	
6	Baseball cap	9,066	£4.99	
7	Fleece	17,369	£14.99	
8				

Formulas Let You Do Calculations

<u>Formulas</u> are the key to doing <u>calculations</u>.
Type an <u>equals sign</u> (=), and then use these basic symbols:

+ (<u>add</u>) **−** (<u>subtract</u>) ***** (<u>multiply</u>) **/** (<u>divide</u>)

To calculate the money made from yellow T-shirts, click in cell D2, and type
= B2 * C2
Then hit return to see the answer.

money made from sales = <u>number sold × selling price</u>

Using a formula means the answer will update itself <u>automatically</u> if you change B2 or C2.

Formulas can even refer to different <u>sheets</u>.
Click on these <u>tabs</u> to see a different sheet.

Relative Cell References Can Change

Relative Cell References are Typed as Normal

In the example above, cell D2 contains the formula "=B2*C2"
— this means "<u>multiply the contents of the two cells on the left</u>".

If you <u>copy</u> cell D2 and <u>paste</u> it into cell D3, the computer usually assumes you <u>still</u> want it to mean "multiply the contents of the two cells on the left" — so it'll <u>actually change</u> the formula to "=B3*C3".

B2 and C2 are called <u>relative cell references</u>.
When you copy and paste them, they <u>change</u> — so that they refer to the <u>same place relative to the new cell</u>.

So if you <u>copy</u> cell D2 and <u>paste</u> it into cells D3 to D7, the revenues from the other types of clothing will be calculated <u>automatically</u>.

	A	B	C	D
	Product name	Number sold	Selling price	Money made from sales
1				
2	Yellow T-shirt	6,753	£6.99	£47,203.47
3	Blue T-shirt	8,115	£6.99	£56,723.85
4	Black T-shirt	11,654	£6.99	£81,461.46
5	Denim shorts	3,420	£9.99	£34,165.80
6	Baseball cap	9,066	£4.99	£45,239.34
7	Fleece	17,369	£14.99	£260,361.31

Sum=£477,951.76

Absolute Cell References Stay Fixed

Sometimes you <u>won't want</u> the computer to <u>change</u> cell references.

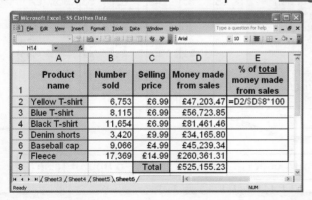

	A	B	C	D	E
	Product name	Number sold	Selling price	Money made from sales	% of total money made from sales
1					
2	Yellow T-shirt	6,753	£6.99	£47,203.47	=D2/D8*100
3	Blue T-shirt	8,115	£6.99	£56,723.85	
4	Black T-shirt	11,654	£6.99	£81,461.46	
5	Denim shorts	3,420	£9.99	£34,165.80	
6	Baseball cap	9,066	£4.99	£45,239.34	
7	Fleece	17,369	£14.99	£260,361.31	
8				Total	£525,155.23

Absolute Cell References Use the $ Symbol

Here, the <u>total</u> sales revenue has been calculated in <u>cell D8</u>, and cell E2 shows the <u>percentage</u> of total revenue made by Yellow T-shirts. So in cell E2 you <u>could</u> type "=D2/D8*100".

<u>But</u>... if you copied and pasted this into cell E3, it would become "=D3/D9*100") — the 'D3' is okay, but the 'D9' will cause problems.

To avoid this, type <u>D8</u> instead — the <u>dollar signs</u> mean the cell reference will stay <u>fixed</u> — it's an <u>absolute cell reference</u>.

When you copy E2 and paste it into cells E3 to E7:
- D8 stays <u>fixed</u> — it's an <u>absolute cell reference</u>.
- D2 <u>changes</u> to D3, D4... — it's a <u>relative cell reference</u>.

I know what you're thinking — this is a formulaic joke...

Formulas are <u>great</u> — if any cells in the formula change, the formula's answers will be updated <u>automatically</u>.
<u>Pasting</u> formulas to other places is cool, but make sure you know when to use <u>absolute cell references</u>.

Spreadsheets: Using Functions

Spreadsheets can be used for basic arithmetic, but there are also <u>functions</u> that allow you to do more complicated calculations in a <u>single step</u>. As always, start with an equals sign '='.

<u>SUM</u> and <u>AVERAGE</u> are Common Functions

~ There's more about this ~
~ in the animated tutorials. ~

This spreadsheet shows the output of five members of staff in a small toy factory.

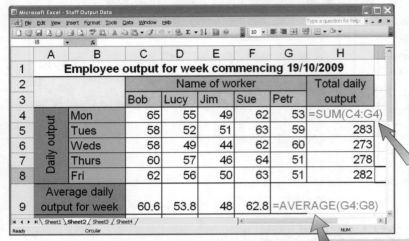

SUM is Used for Adding

The <u>SUM</u>() function <u>adds</u> the contents of whatever <u>cells</u> you put in the brackets.

E.g. to find the <u>total</u> output of all five staff on <u>Monday</u> (row 4), you <u>could</u> enter:
= SUM(C4, D4, E4, F4, G4)

But it's quicker to type a <u>range</u> of cells using a colon (:). You could do the above calculation as:
= SUM(C4 : G4)

AVERAGE, MIN and MAX — also useful

The <u>AVERAGE</u>() function finds the <u>mean</u> of whatever cells you put in the brackets.
The <u>MIN</u>() and <u>MAX</u>() functions can be used to work out the smallest and biggest numbers in a set of data.

To find <u>Petr's</u> average daily output, enter:
= AVERAGE(G4 : G8)

If you use <u>relative</u> cell references, you can fill in the other totals and averages by pasting the functions (see the previous page).

IF Checks to See if Conditions Have Been Met

The managers now want to check whether each worker's average output is meeting the target of <u>over 54 toys per day</u>. If it is, the cell in row 10 under their name should say "Yes". If not, it should say "No".

IF Checks Whether Something is True

You can set the <u>IF</u>() function to <u>output</u> different results depending on whether a condition is <u>true or false</u>.

To test whether Bob's average output (cell C9) is <u>greater than 54</u>, type in cell C10:
= IF(C9 > 54, "Yes", "No")
Bob's average is 60.6, so the output is "Yes".

But when you paste the function into Lucy's column (cell D10), the output is "No", since her average output for the week is <u>less than</u> 54.

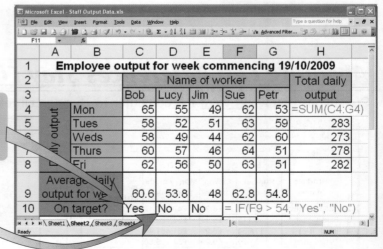

This is a tricky one — the basic form is: =IF(condition to check, "output if true", "output if false")

I used the SUM function — now everything adds up...

Functions can look a bit off-putting at first, but once you've used them a couple of times you'll never go back to typing sums and averages the long way. Functions can use <u>absolute</u> and <u>relative</u> cell references, too. Just remember that you still need to use an <u>equals sign</u> before your function name. <u>Practice</u> is key here.

Spreadsheets: Graphs and Charts

Graphs and charts are ways of communicating data visually. Spreadsheets are great at turning dull numbers into colourful diagrams — they do most of the hard work for you.

Bar Charts are Often Called Column Charts

See the animated tutorials for more information.

The owners of the Broken Chair café have made a spreadsheet of their drinks sales.
They want to produce a bar chart to show how their sales of hot drinks compare over a year.

Microsoft Excel - Drinks Sales Data.xls

		Mar 2008 – May 2008	Jun 2008 – Aug 2008	Sep 2008 – Nov 2008	Dec 2008 – Feb 2009	
1	Drinks sales at the Broken Chair Café March 2008 – Feb 2009					
3	Tea	2468	2736	3064	3320	11588
4	Coffee	2654	2003	2803	3586	11046
5	Hot choc	2120	1506	2187	2648	8461
6	OJ	2355	3112	1981	1094	8542
7	Lemonade	1862	2917	1631	906	7316
8	Cola	2135	3365	1938	963	8401
9	Total	13594	15639	13604	12517	55354

First Select Your Data

Select the cells that contain the data you want to display in your chart. Include any headings.

You can sometimes select groups of cells that aren't next to each other by holding down the Ctrl key.

Then Create Your Chart

There will probably be loads of ways you could do this, and masses of options you can play with.

This is what you get using the basic bar chart (or column chart in some spreadsheets) option.

Your headings are used in the legend (or key) — this tells you which column is which.

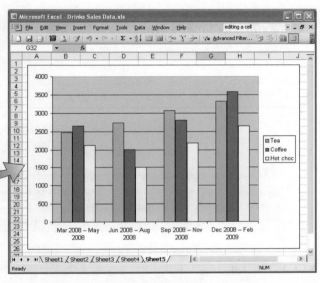

Finally, Edit Your Chart Till it Shines

You can adjust pretty much every part of a chart. Use the chart menus, or try right-clicking on different parts to see the options.

Remember to add a title and put labels on axes. You can choose the font, size and colour of the text.

You can also change the colours used, the style and thickness of lines, and the range of values shown on each axis.

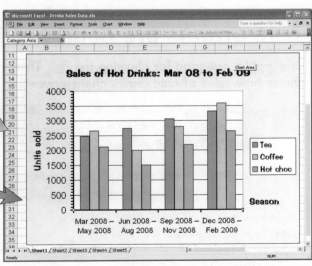

Don't get carried away with editing your charts. Remember that in business, it's more important to show data clearly than to make it look pretty.

Produce the best charts bar none...

A lot of spreadsheets have wizards that will help you draw graphs and charts. You normally have to answer a few questions, select some cells when it tells you to, and the wizard will sort out the rest. If you use the wizard to draw the chart in the first place, you can always customise it later to make it sparkle.

Spreadsheets: Graphs and Charts

Whatever kind of chart you want to make, the basic technique is the same — <u>select</u> the data series, choose the <u>chart type</u>, then <u>edit</u> it until it looks the way you want it to.

See the animated tutorials for more about charts and graphs.

Pie Charts **Show** Proportions

The owners of the café now want to look at their drinks sales for Dec 2008 – Feb 2009. They want to see what <u>proportion</u> of their total sales for this period came from each drink.

Select the Data You Need

Pie charts show data as slices of a round pie. To create one, highlight the <u>data</u> plus any <u>headings</u>.

If the data you need isn't in one block (like here, where the data is in columns B and F)... ...select the first group of cells (e.g. column B), then <u>hold down ctrl</u> and select the second group (column F).

Pie Charts Come in Different Flavours

Basic pie charts are <u>circles</u> split into sectors. But spreadsheets often let you go to town... ...and make 3D pies with slices exploding outwards. The main thing is to make the chart <u>clear</u>.

This pie chart was made using the <u>chart wizard</u>, but it's been <u>tweaked</u> a bit.

Sometimes, it's easier to read a <u>label</u> than use a <u>legend</u>. You can usually choose from different options — these labels show the <u>percentages</u> of total sales, but you could show the <u>original data</u> if you prefer.

You can also change things like the <u>colours</u> and <u>sizes</u> of the slices, and <u>how far apart</u> they've exploded.

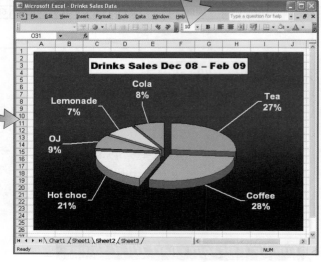

Line Graphs **are Good for Showing** Changes Over Time

Line graphs are good for showing <u>trends</u>. This graph shows how sales of cold drinks <u>change</u> over the year.

You could show this information in a bar chart. But lines sometimes show the ups and downs a bit more clearly if you're looking at a <u>long period</u>, or you have <u>lots of data points</u>.

Here, it's pretty clear that sales of all three cold drinks <u>peak</u> in August, and <u>fall steadily</u> towards winter.

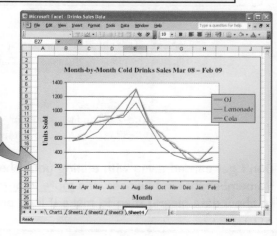

Before printing, an on-screen "print preview" will show you <u>exactly</u> how the printout will look. You can then:
• change the <u>page orientation</u>: 'portrait' — ☐, or 'landscape' — ▭,
• change where the <u>page-breaks</u> fall,
• include (or turn off) <u>grid lines</u>.

Yeah, I traded laughs / In for chartsengrafs...

Once you've got data in a spreadsheet, producing professional-looking charts and graphs is a piece of cake. Or a slice of pie. The important thing is to make sure that your choice of chart is <u>appropriate</u> for your data.

Revision Summary for Section Eight

Another practical section under your belt. Well, nearly, anyway. There's still the tricky matter of the Revision Summary to negotiate. As always, try the questions below (including all the practical ones), and see how you do. You're aiming for 100% success, so if you get anything wrong, go back and look those bits up, then have another go.

1) A spreadsheet looks like a big grid, made up of individual cells.
How are each of these individual cells referenced?

2) What is a 'validation rule' for a cell's contents?

3) What does it mean to merge two cells together?

4) What is conditional formatting?
How do you set conditional formats in your spreadsheet software?

5) What would you type into a cell to add the contents of cells A1 and H6?
What formula would you type to multiply the contents of cells A1 and H6?
What would you type to divide the contents of cell H6 by the contents of cell A1?

6) In a spreadsheet, what's the difference between an absolute cell reference and a relative cell reference?

7) a) Copy the table on the right into a spreadsheet.

b) Use a formula and relative cell references to fill in the profits for 2006 to 2009 in column D (profit = money received – money spent).

c) Use functions and relative cell references to fill in the totals and averages for columns B, C and D.

d) Use conditional formatting in column D so that any negative figures automatically appear in red. Change cell B5 to 50 to check you've done this okay.

e) Add an IF() function to cell D8.
• If the average profit figure in cell D7 is less than 10, then your IF() function should output "Oh dear".
• If the average profit figure in cell D7 is 10 or over, your IF() function should output "Grand".
• Change cell B5 back to 140 to check you've done this okay.

	A	B	C	D
1		Money received (£000s)	Money spent (£000s)	Profit (£000s)
2	2006	120	80	
3	2007	82	139	
4	2008	129	82	
5	2009	140	76	
6	Total			
7	Average			

8) a) Use the data from Q7 to produce a line graph showing how money received, money spent and profits changed between 2006 and 2009.

b) Add a title, labels, and a legend, and adjust the colours so that your graph is thoroughly pleasing.

c) Insert your chart into a blank word processor document.

Answers to Q7 b) and c)

	Money received (£000s)	Money spent (£000s)	Profit (£000s)
2006	120	80	40
2007	82	135	53
2008	129	82	47
2009	140	76	64
Total	524	320	204
Average	131	80	51

Databases

Databases are mostly used for storing a <u>mixture</u> of data — it might be names, addresses, reference numbers, dates, financial figures... you name it. The easiest way to think of a database is as a glorified <u>table</u>.

Databases Store All Kinds of Data

 The animated tutorial will take you through this stuff step by step.

Flat-File Databases Store Data in One Table

Databases organise information in tables with <u>rows</u> and <u>columns</u>. A <u>flat-file</u> database contains <u>one</u> table.

Each row is a separate <u>record</u>. Each record contains data about <u>one</u> person or item.

Databases often have a <u>key field</u> that <u>uniquely</u> <u>identifies</u> each record. Here there's a field called 'ID' — this is a <u>different</u> number for every record.

The column headings are <u>field names</u> — a <u>field</u> is just a <u>particular</u> <u>category of data</u> in the table (e.g. name, telephone number).

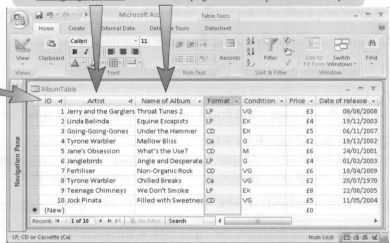

Relational Databases Contain Linked Tables

<u>Relational</u> databases organise data in <u>several</u> tables, where each table stores a <u>different</u> <u>type</u> of information. But <u>links</u> between <u>related</u> <u>tables</u> can be made using their <u>key fields</u>.

Relational databases are much more <u>useful</u> than flat-file databases. But they can be <u>difficult</u> to set up if you're not a database pro.

Records Can be Edited...

- To <u>edit</u> (change) a record, just click in a cell and type over the old data.

...and Deleted

- To <u>delete</u> a record, click somewhere in it and then click on the delete button.

You Can Set Data Types and Options in the Design View

Databases usually have a '<u>design view</u>' as well. This is where you 'set up' your table.

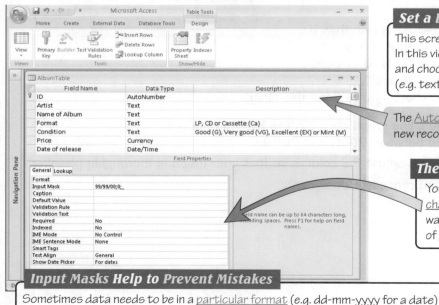

Set a Data Type for Each Field

This screen shows the <u>design view</u> of a database table. In this view you can change the <u>names</u> of your fields, and choose what <u>type</u> of data will be listed in each field (e.g. text, number, date, currency).

The <u>Autonumber</u> data type automatically gives each new record a different number — good for <u>key fields</u>.

There are Options for Each Data Type

You can set the <u>maximum number of</u> <u>characters</u> each entry can contain, and the way the data is <u>displayed</u> (e.g. the number of <u>decimal places</u>, or a <u>currency</u> symbol).

Encoding Data Can Save Time

You can give data values a short <u>code</u> to <u>save time</u> typing them out in full every time. E.g. 'North' could be encoded as 'N'.

Input Masks Help to Prevent Mistakes

Sometimes data needs to be in a <u>particular format</u> (e.g. dd-mm-yyyy for a date) — <u>input masks</u> make sure that data can <u>only</u> be entered in this format.

I remember when all this was fields...

<u>Flat-file</u> databases are great for <u>simple</u> sets of data — it's easy to handle data contained in a <u>single table</u>. But for a firm that stores more <u>complex</u> data, a <u>relational</u> database may increase <u>efficiency</u>.

Databases: Data Input Forms

Think of a database as being a bit like a swan (no, don't roll your eyes skywards... work with me a bit). The tables are the bits that do all the work but which are not great looking — so tables are a swan's legs. Forms are the pretty bits that are on show — the bit of a swan above the water. There... clear as anything.

Forms Are a User-Friendly Way to Enter Data

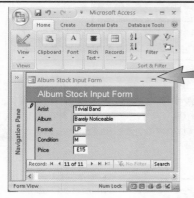

The animated tutorial will take you through designing a form step by step.

Forms Should be Clear and Simple

- Forms can be used to enter data into a table. The idea is that they're clearly designed and user-friendly to make this as easy as possible.

Forms can contain text boxes (for typing into), or tick-boxes and 'option lists' for users to choose from. You can even display input masks in your text boxes.

When a user has entered their data, it's stored as a new record in the database table.

Forms and Tables Can be Linked

Choose a Table

When you create a form, you have to decide which table new data will end up in.

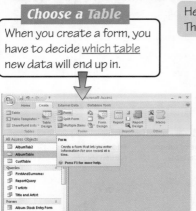

Here, the form has been used to enter a new record into the table. The details in this form will form the 11th row in this table.

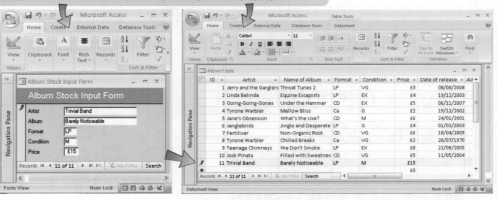

Use the Form Design View to Adjust Links and Layout

You Can Edit the Design of Forms

Like tables, forms have a design view where you can change their layout and appearance. You need to make your forms clear and logical so users know exactly what data they're being asked for.

You can add text boxes and labels using the design view.
- Text boxes are linked to fields.
- Labels are there just to help users understand the form.

You can also adjust the colours, fonts, and borders used on your form.

Text boxes need to be linked to fields in a table. But you don't have to include every field from the table in your form.

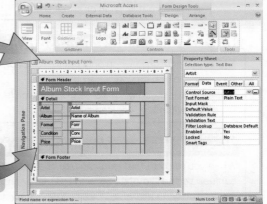

I'm a confused input form — can you fill me in?

Forms are supposed to be the friendly face of a database. A good form should make it obvious what data is needed, and be easy to use. If a form isn't clear, there's more chance that data will be entered incorrectly.

Databases: Simple Queries and Sorting

Databases can quickly <u>sort</u> data into <u>order</u>. They can also quickly find all the records that meet <u>certain</u> <u>conditions</u> (e.g. all your friends who are taller than 6 feet). It's a lot handier than I'm making it sound.

Data Can be Sorted Into Order by Field

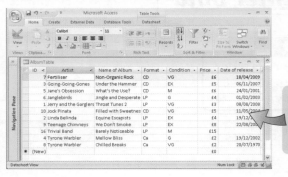

Sorting Data Means Changing its Order

When you add records to a database, they'll be listed in the <u>order</u> <u>you typed them</u>. But it's easy to <u>sort</u> data into a more useful order.

For example, the records in this table have been sorted into <u>alphabetical</u> <u>order</u> using the 'Artist' field. To sort your records, click somewhere in the field you want to put in order, and click on the '<u>sort ascending</u>' button. You can sort in the <u>opposite order</u> by choosing '<u>sort descending</u>'.

Queries are Used to Search and Filter Data

The animated tutorial will walk you through a query.

Queries Let You Filter Out the Data You Want

This is the <u>query design</u> screen. A query lets you look for records whose entries meet certain conditions — this is called <u>filtering</u>. Choose the <u>fields</u> you're interested in, and the <u>criteria</u> you want to search for.

You can also choose how you want the results to be <u>sorted</u>, and which fields you want to <u>show</u> in the results.

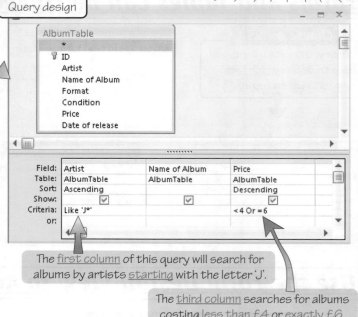

Query design

Tips for Query Criteria

Use 'Quotes' for Words

If you're searching for a <u>word</u>, put <u>quotes</u> around it in the criteria box — e.g. 'apple' or 'Smith'.

=, < and > are Useful for Queries

These symbols let you search for a <u>range</u> of data.
= (<u>equal to</u>)   < (<u>less than</u>)   > (<u>greater than</u>)
<> (<u>not equal to</u>)   <= (<u>less than or equal to</u>)
>= (<u>greater than or equal to</u>)

The <u>first column</u> of this query will search for albums by artists <u>starting</u> with the letter 'J'.

The <u>third column</u> searches for albums costing <u>less than £4</u> or <u>exactly £6</u>.

Use Like and * for Wildcard Searches

A <u>wildcard search</u> is when only <u>part</u> of a record has to match your search criteria.
For example, if you want to search for words <u>ending</u> with 'ity', you can type Like '*ity'.

So the <u>query results</u> will display albums by artists starting with 'J' <u>and</u> costing either <u>less than £4</u> or <u>exactly £6</u>.

Use Logic for More Complex Searches

When you're confident you can use the basics, you can use terms like <u>AND</u>, <u>OR</u> and <u>NOT</u> to search for several criteria at once. (See the next page too.)

Query results

There's nowt so queries folk...

Queries are just <u>questions</u>. You can ask a database to display data that satisfies <u>particular criteria</u>, which saves loads of time wading through the records. Make sure you're happy with all this before your exam.

Databases: Producing Reports

You can fill a database with stacks of information, but reading from the table can be like solving a very big, very dull wordsearch. Reports can be used to display data in a way that will make your eyes explode with joy.

Reports Are Linked to Tables or Queries

Reports can present data so it's both beautiful and easy to understand.
Reports can be designed to be viewed on screen or printed out.

Reports Display Data

You can base reports on either tables or queries.

It depends on whether you need to display all the records in a table, or just the ones that meet certain conditions.

This query uses two lines to specify the search criteria instead of using 'OR'. You'd get the same result by putting ">2 OR <10" in the Price field.

This is the report based on the query on the left. There's a bit of colour and text formatting, and a title to make it clear what the report shows.

Design Reports to be Clear and Attractive

This is the design view of the report above.

Link Reports to Data Sources

Producing a report has a lot in common with producing a form (see p69).
1) Choose a data source (usually a table or a query).
2) Link the text boxes to fields in your data source (in the design view).
3) Make it look lovely.

Give your report a title that tells the reader what the report is saying.

This is just a label that appears on every page.

This text box is linked to a field — the information shown in it will be different on every line of the report.

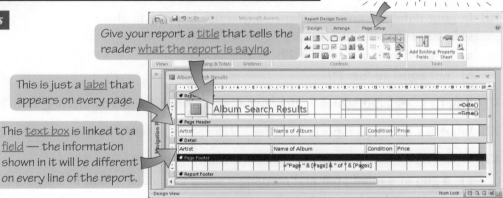

Wizards Can Make Forms, Reports and Queries Easier

Wizards Can Make Life Easier

Designing a decent-looking form/query/report from scratch can take time. A lot of programs have wizards that help make the process less painful.

You usually answer a series of questions, and the wizard sorts out the technical details. You can always adjust the details afterwards using design view.

Linking reports to tables — it's as sourcey as DBs get...

You won't be asked to produce a really complicated report in the exam, but it's well worth knowing your way around the basic techniques. Oh, and remember to use a suitable title. And, er, that's about it for databases.

Revision Summary for Section Nine

A short and sweet section for you. But a tricky one, I reckon. Databases look like they should be easy to use, but they can be stroppy, and suddenly refuse to do things for no apparent reason (or maybe they just do that to me). What I usually do in those circumstances is shout at the screen a bit, then get a cup of tea, and come back 20 minutes later when I've calmed down.
But this won't be an option in your Exam, so you need to make extra double sure you can get the database to do the things you need to. That's where these questions will come in handy. You know the drill... try them all, and if you get any wrong, revise those bits till you can get the question right.

1) In a database, what's the difference between a field and a record?

2) What's the basic difference between a relational database and a flat-file database?

3) How can using a key field ensure that every record in a database table is unique?

4) What is meant by a 'data type'? Name three data types.

5) What is an input mask, and why might you use one?

6) Explain the reasons for using a form to input data into a table, instead of entering data directly into the table.

7) On a form, what's the difference between a text box and a label?

8) What does it mean to 'sort' data?

9) What can a database query be used to do?

10) In your database software, how do you use a query to show only records with entries in a particular field that are:
   a) greater than or equal to 5?
   b) not equal to 'basil'?

11) What's a wildcard search? How would you search for words starting with 'be'?

12) What are database reports used for? Name two possible data sources for a report.

13) Which of the following best defines a wizard?
   a) a guy in a pointy hat and carrying a wand who does a load of magic and stuff.
   b) a series of dialogues that allows a computer user to easily perform a complex task.

14) a) Create a database table containing these fields: first name, surname, gender, date of birth. Include a suitable input mask for the 'date of birth' field.
   b) Design a form for inputting data into this table.
   c) Use the form to enter your details. Then enter details for five people who are older than you, and five people who are younger (you can make them up).
   d) Design a query to display all the people who were born after your birthday, so that the results are sorted in ascending alphabetical order by surname.
   e) Design a report to display the results of this query in a stylish way. Print it out and treasure it.

Graphics: Creating Images

This section rounds up some more software applications that businesses often use. Starting with graphics...

Images — Either Bitmaps or Vector Drawings

These two basic types of graphic are stored and edited in different ways.

BITMAPS — these can be made and edited with 'Painting' software.
Digital photographs and scanned images are often stored as bitmaps.

1) A bitmap image is made up of a grid of coloured dots (pixels). Bitmap files take up a lot of memory because data is stored for every individual pixel.

2) To edit the image, you have to alter the individual dots (although bitmap-editing software has lots of different tools to make this easier).

VECTOR GRAPHICS — these are made with 'Drawing' software.

Bitmaps can be made up of thousands of these coloured dots — if you zoom right in, you can see them.

1) A vector image is stored as coordinates and equations — making file sizes a lot smaller. (But when you're making or editing a vector image, you never have to use equations — the software takes care of all those. You only ever have to use the software's drawing tools.)

2) You create or edit images by manipulating various lines and geometric shapes (simple shapes like squares and circles, or very complicated ones). You can stretch them, twist them, colour them, and so on.

Graphics Packages Help You Create and Edit Images

Vector-based graphics are usually made up of loads of separate lines and shapes.
These individual objects can be moved, resized, or copied independently. Here's a few things you can do...

Straight lines and freehand lines can be drawn with different properties — thickness, style and colour can be changed.

Vector software has tools to draw simple shapes like squares, rectangles, circles, triangles, and so on. You can then edit these basic shapes to make arrows, speech bubbles and other more complex designs.

Fill and shading tools let you change the colours and backgrounds of objects. You can have faded or patterned fills as well as single colours.

The text tool lets you add writing to your graphics. You can often add borders and shading to text, and bend it into shapes.

You can change the size of any object by dragging one of the handles (around the outside of the image) outwards or inwards. But if you don't keep the proportions the same, you can end up with very stretched or squashed images.

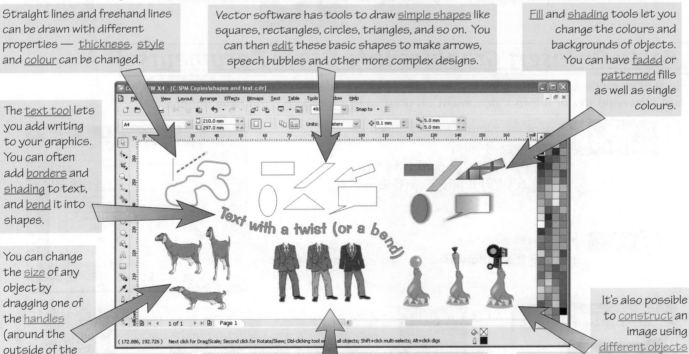

Because most vector graphics (except basic shapes) consist of separate objects, it's easy to change the colour of certain parts of the graphic, like this jacket and trousers, by recolouring individual objects.

It's also possible to construct an image using different objects — the seal originally balanced a ball but that part of the graphic can be removed and replaced with pretty much anything.

Picture this — being tested while sat at a computer...

I like drawing pictures. I like all the pretty colours. Anyway, enough of that... get yourself sat down in front of a computer and make sure you can do all the things on this page. If you're not sure how, ask someone.

Graphics: Manipulating Images

There's still a bit more about graphics you need to know. And here it is.

See the animated tutorial too.

Cropping Removes Unwanted Bits of Pictures

Cropping is dead useful when you need to make a picture <u>fill a hole</u> in your document perfectly.

1) <u>Cropping</u> removes parts of the image you don't want — e.g. someone on the edge of the shot you want to get rid of. Cropping can reduce the size of the image by removing blocks from the <u>edges</u>.

2) It's <u>quick</u> and <u>easy</u>, although it can only remove whole <u>edges</u> — you can't use it to remove something in the <u>middle</u> of the graphic. (There's usually a separate tool for this.)

For example, suppose you've written a newsletter article, but your picture <u>just doesn't fit</u>...

① Suppose you need to get this photo in that gap.

② It's the right width, but way too tall.

③ Don't need all that sky, so crop some off.

④ Smashing.

3) Cropping is often a better way to make a picture fit a hole, rather than <u>stretching</u> or <u>squashing</u> it.

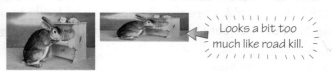

Looks a bit too much like road kill.

Paste Or Insert Graphics Into Other Documents

So you've made a beautiful <u>graphic</u>. But maybe you made it in a <u>graphics program</u>, and now need to get it into a document on your <u>word processor</u>. You have options...

① **Copy and Paste**
- <u>Select</u> the picture in your piece of graphics software.
- <u>Copy</u> it to the clipboard (Ctrl C).
- <u>Paste</u> (Ctrl V) it into your document.

② **Insert**
- <u>Save</u> your picture.
- <u>Insert</u> the picture file.

A lot of programs have an Insert menu. Find your picture, and Bob's your uncle.

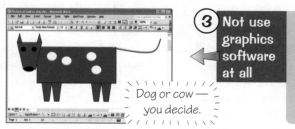

Dog or cow — you decide.

③ **Not use graphics software at all**
- A lot of software (e.g. some word processors, spreadsheets etc.) lets you make <u>basic</u> pictures <u>without</u> using special graphics software (see p58).
- This is best for quite <u>simple</u> graphics. For anything <u>fancy</u>, you're probably better off using a proper <u>painting</u> or <u>drawing</u> program.

So that's why newspaper pictures always fit the gaps...

You'd have quite a time trying to make a newspaper without the <u>crop tool</u> — it's dead handy, and a lot of <u>word processors</u> will have one. Give it a go. No I mean it, give it a go and make sure you can do it.

Presentation Software

<u>Presentations</u> are used for giving oral information to an audience, all gift-wrapped in visual loveliness.

Presentations Combine Oral and Visual Communication

1) Presentations are used to <u>communicate</u> information to an <u>audience</u>, or to <u>persuade</u> them of something. Usually there's a <u>speaker</u>, and they might have some equipment or props to help them. For example...

| Flipcharts |
These are big pieces of <u>paper</u> on a pad — the speaker can flip from page to page. They're okay for a <u>small room</u>, but harder for a large audience to see.

| Overhead transparencies (OHTs): |
These are clear plastic sheets — the contents can be <u>projected</u> onto a screen. The <u>size</u> of the image can be adjusted, so they're better for <u>large audiences</u>. You can <u>print</u> transparencies from a computer or write them <u>by hand</u>.

| Slideshows |
These are usually made using <u>presentation software</u> — an LCD <u>projector</u> can be used to display a series of <u>slides</u> while the speaker gives their talk.

2) The idea is that the <u>visual</u> material (slides, OHTs, or whatever) help to <u>support</u> the spoken information.

Presentations made on a computer can look more <u>professional</u> than hand-written materials.

Presentation Software Uses Tools Like a Word Processor

Presentation software creates a series of <u>slides</u> in a single document. You can design your slides <u>from scratch</u>, or you can use a <u>template</u>. Either way, you can <u>edit the layout</u> with a range of tools and objects.

Text is Typed in Text Boxes...
...no surprises there. You can use all the usual <u>text formatting</u> options in a text box.

<u>Bullet points</u> are especially handy in presentations, since they split text into <u>bite-size chunks</u> of info. Plus, you can make bullet points appear on a slide <u>one at a time</u>.

You Can Add Notes to Slides
Notes aren't displayed on the slide, but they can be printed and used to <u>remind</u> the speaker about <u>key points</u> during the presentation.

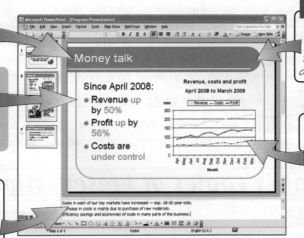

Use Colour Effectively
You can set the <u>background</u> colour for your slides, and use coloured <u>shapes</u>, <u>boxes</u>, <u>lines</u> and <u>borders</u> to draw attention to parts of the slide.

Insert Pictures Wisely
You can put <u>pictures</u>, <u>charts</u> or <u>tables</u> into slides.

Sometimes you can make these in the <u>presentation software</u>.

You can also insert <u>pictures</u> from <u>clip art</u>, or another source (e.g. a graphics package).

Use Effects to Add Movement to Your Slides

See the animated tutorial too.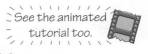

1) **TIMINGS** Presentation software lets you decide <u>when</u> objects will <u>appear</u> on the slide. For example, each bullet point in a list can appear at just the right moment, or when you click the mouse.

2) **ANIMATION EFFECTS** can be used to make objects <u>move</u> on the screen in <u>eye-catching ways</u>.
   • For example, a line of <u>text</u> can appear one word at a time, or the <u>size</u> and <u>style</u> of the font can change.
   • A picture can <u>grow</u>, <u>shrink</u>, <u>rotate</u>, or <u>move around</u> along a set path.

3) **TRANSITIONS** are effects that come in when you change from <u>one slide to the next</u>. For example, new slides can fly in from one side of the screen, or the slides can 'open and close' like shutters or curtains.

Everything's on the slide...

Presentation software is a useful tool, but it's best to <u>keep things simple</u>. Don't get <u>carried away</u> with jazzy effects — a lot of them can end up looking a bit... silly. There's more about all this on the next page.

Presentations

So, presentation software can do all kinds of exciting stuff. But it's <u>not always</u> the best option — you need to choose the <u>most appropriate method</u> to give an effective presentation.

Remember the Rules for Giving a Good Presentation

1) `CHOOSE THE BEST EQUIPMENT` — it's not always best to use fancy hi-tech presentation software.

- Presentation software is great for making slides look <u>professional</u> — it's usually the best choice for <u>large companies</u> with a strong <u>corporate image</u>.
- It's also good for making <u>attention-grabbing</u> presentations — animations and clever timings can help to keep an audience interested (and you can't use these on paper or OHTs).
- But electronic <u>hardware</u> (e.g. computers and projectors) and <u>software</u> can be <u>pricey</u> — a flipchart/OHT approach might be more cost-effective for small firms.
- <u>Technical issues</u> can also cause problems — it's important to <u>test</u> electronic presentations using the hardware that will be used in the <u>presentation</u>. E.g. large movie clips might run very slowly on some systems — it's <u>embarrassing</u> for the speaker if things don't go as planned.

2) `REMEMBER YOUR AUDIENCE` — the wrong choice of presentation technique can put people off.

- A large company giving a presentation to important <u>stakeholders</u> would probably use an electronic slideshow with charts and diagrams. (Handwritten slides would look a bit shoddy in this situation.)
- For a <u>small</u>, <u>informal</u> presentation, a flipchart might be better — especially since you can <u>add extra ideas</u> from the audience to a flipchart as you go along.

3) `DON'T OVERLOAD YOUR SLIDES` with <u>too much information</u>. A good slide should only contain a few <u>short points</u> and possibly a diagram — much more will <u>distract</u> the audience from the <u>talk</u>. As a general rule, you should aim to talk for at least <u>two minutes</u> for each of your slides.

4) `USE CONSISTENT SLIDES` — using a similar <u>style</u> and <u>layout</u> on each slide often looks more <u>professional</u>.

5) `USE PICTURES AND DIAGRAMS` if they'll help. A picture can speak a thousand words, after all. And remember that <u>charts</u> are really good for showing patterns and trends in a set of figures.

Handouts are Paper Copies of Presentation Materials

Print Your Slides as Handouts

Presentation software allows speakers to print their slides and give them to the audience as <u>handouts</u> so they can <u>make notes</u> on them during the presentation and refer to them <u>afterwards</u>.

You can set the print options to display <u>several slides</u> on one page — this <u>saves paper</u>, and the text should be large enough to read if the slides are well designed.

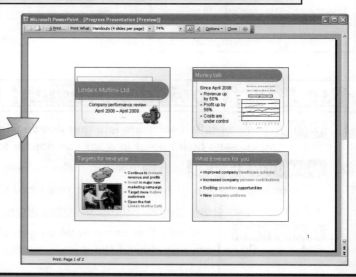

1) Handouts <u>don't</u> have to be made using presentation software.
2) They could be <u>photocopies</u> of OHTs, or <u>extra information</u> that might be useful.

Hold your handout — I've got a present(ation) for you...

There are lots of factors to keep in mind when planning a presentation. The best method to use depends on the <u>situation</u> and the <u>audience</u> — there's no point making things <u>more complicated</u> than they need to be.

Web-Authoring Software

You can create simple web pages using a word processor.
But web-authoring software can make it easier to put a complex web site together.

Web-Authoring Software is a Bit Like a Word Processor...

For the most part, using web-authoring software is similar to using a word processor.
You can add text, pictures and so on in much the same way.

See the animated tutorial too.

It's a good idea to use a similar 'look' on every page of a website...

Keep menus in the same place on each page to make it easier to navigate.

Make the page headings match the menu options.

Use a similar colour scheme on each page (you could always vary the colour scheme between different sections of the site).

Text should be easy to read on-screen.

The look of a business website should suit the business's image — see p47.

Borders and lines can help break up the page.

You can animate things to make them more eye-catching.

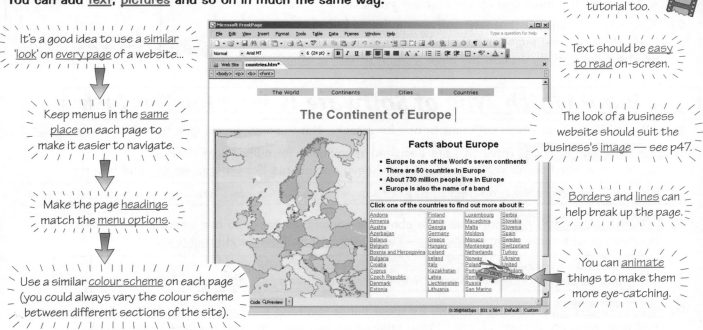

...With Some Important Differences

1) Any object on a webpage can be turned into a 'clickable' hyperlink to take you to a different page.
2) You can even make several links on the same image using 'hotspots'.
   For example, clicking on each town on this map might take you to a page about that town.

Think of the users when you're choosing graphics...

...high-resolution images look better on screen but they can take ages to download.

...low-resolution images download quicker, but can become pixelated (blocky).

Frames allow different parts of the webpage to work independently. Here, when the user scrolls down the main part of the page, the top frame remains visible.

Frames allow you to keep useful buttons and menus on the screen at all times. But on small screens (e.g. PDAs and Smartphones), there's often not enough space for frames to work properly.

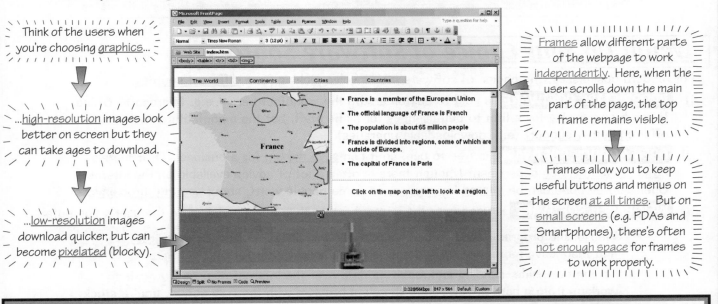

After this summer's washout, I'm in need of a hotspot...

Frames are a bit 'last year' really — not a lot of sites use them these days. But they're mentioned on the exam specification, so make sure you know how to use them in whatever software you're using. It's adding hyperlinks between pages that you might need to practise — try it in a word processor if you need to.

DTP and Evaluating Software

Nearly there now — just one more type of software to mention, then you can get on with some <u>evaluating</u>.

DTP _is Like a Frame-Based Word Processor_

1) <u>Desk top publishing</u> (<u>DTP</u>) software has <u>a lot in common</u> with a word processor — you can use it to combine <u>text and graphics</u> on a page, and most of the tools and options are very similar.

2) The main difference is that DTP software is <u>frame based</u>. Each object on the page is contained in its own frame (or box), which can be moved <u>freely</u> around the page <u>without affecting other frames</u>.

Evaluate _Which Type of Software is Best for the Task_

Sometimes it's obvious which software to use for a task. But in some cases, you have to make a <u>choice</u>...

1) `WORD PROCESSORS` (p56-60) are designed specifically for editing <u>text</u> (words). You'd use a word processor to produce text-heavy documents like <u>letters</u>, <u>memos</u> and <u>reports</u>.

> Word processors can combine text with <u>pictures</u> to produce more complex documents. But it's not always the best option...

2) `DESK TOP PUBLISHING` software (see above) is sometimes easier to use when you're making documents with more <u>complex layouts</u> — e.g. <u>newsletters</u>, <u>flyers</u> and <u>brochures</u>.

> This is because DTP software is <u>frame based</u> — it's easy to move text, graphics, and other objects around the page <u>separately</u>. With a word processor, moving one object can make <u>everything else</u> on the page move as well.

3) `SPREADSHEETS` (p62-66) are ideal for most things involving <u>numbers</u> — e.g. doing <u>calculations</u>, and producing <u>graphs</u> and <u>charts</u>. Many businesses use them to keep track of <u>financial data</u>.

> Spreadsheets can also be used to <u>organise</u> other types of data (e.g. text) into <u>tables</u>. But databases give you more options...

4) `DATABASES` (p68-71) are great for <u>storing</u> and <u>processing</u> large amounts of data — <u>text</u>, <u>numbers</u>, <u>dates</u>... you name it. You can <u>search</u> a database to pick out <u>exactly</u> the information you want, so businesses often use them to store things like <u>customer details</u> and <u>market research information</u>.

> The main problem is that databases can be <u>complicated</u> to set up and use, especially relational databases.

Weigh Up Your Choice of Software Sources

For modern businesses, the choice of software may involve picking from <u>different sources</u>.

1) `PROPRIETARY SOFTWARE` is <u>sold</u> to customers by the manufacturer — e.g. Microsoft® Office. It can be <u>expensive</u> for a firm to buy <u>licences</u> for all its staff, but the manufacturer will often offer <u>customer support</u> (e.g. downloadable upgrades).

2) `OPEN-SOURCE SOFTWARE` is <u>free</u> to use, so it can <u>save money</u> for a business. But there's <u>no customer service</u> department (though there is often a lot of advice available on the internet). Open-source code can be <u>altered</u> by <u>anyone</u>, so some people worry about <u>security problems</u>.

3) `WEB-BASED SOFTWARE` is used <u>over the internet</u> rather than being <u>installed</u> on the user's computer.

- Web-based programs tend to be <u>cheaper</u> than installed software (or even <u>free</u>), and they leave more storage space free on your computer for <u>other uses</u>.

- On the downside, sending and receiving data over the internet may be <u>slower</u> than working from a hard drive. And if there's a <u>problem</u> with the <u>connection</u>, you're stuck.

See you later, evaluator...

Not surprisingly, different software packages are designed to do <u>different tasks</u>. It's worth remembering that you can often make different packages <u>work together</u> by <u>importing</u> objects from one package into another.

Revision Summary for Section Ten

That was the last section in the book, so I'll keep this brief — you should know what you're doing by now. Grab yourself a pen, a computer, and a selection of software, and away you go.

1) Explain the main differences between bitmap and vector graphics.

2) Use a graphics package for this question and the next one.
    a) Put these shapes into a new file: a circle, a triangle, a rectangle, and... a freehand star.
    b) Shade each shape a different colour. Give the rectangle a blue dashed outline.
    c) Try to stay awake. Find some vector clip art of a penguin, and put it on the page.
    d) Resize your circle so that it's a bit taller than the penguin (but still a circle, not an oval).
    e) Put the circle behind the penguin. Use the text tool to add a humorous speech bubble.

3) a) When manipulating images, what is meant by cropping?
    b) Find a bitmap photo of a building with lots of sky in the background. Crop out most of the sky.
    c) Save your cropped picture as 'building' and insert it into a new word processor file.

4) Describe two ways that you could transfer a picture from your graphics package into your word-processor.

5) Discuss the pros and cons that using presentation software might have for a business.

6) Describe three types of equipment that a person could use when giving a presentation.

7) Give three features of a good presentation slide.

8) What is meant by a 'transition' in presentation software?

9) Why should you always test any equipment that's going to be used during a presentation?

10) Explain five things that can have an impact on the look and feel of a website.

11) What does the word 'pixelated' mean?

12) What's the purpose of using frames on a website? Give a disadvantage of using frames.

13) Explain the main difference between a desk top publishing package and a word processor.

14) Describe the differences between proprietary and open-source software.

15) Give one advantage and one disadvantage of using software over the internet.

Controlled Assessment

Assessment — what a <u>nightmare</u>. Well... it certainly will be if you don't know what to expect.
If you <u>do</u> know what to expect then it's a lot less scary.

Your Assessment Will Be in Three Parts

The AQA assessment is in <u>three</u> very <u>different</u> stages.

①   **A 1-hour <u>Written Paper</u> on Unit 8 — ICT Systems in Business.
Worth <u>40%</u> of your GCSE.**

②   **A 1½-hour <u>Computer-Based Examination</u> on Unit 9 — Using ICT in Business.
Worth <u>35%</u> of your GCSE.**

③   **A <u>Controlled Assessment</u> on Unit 10 — Investigating ICT in Business.
Worth <u>25%</u> of your GCSE.**

Controlled Assessment Tasks are Quite "Open"

1)   You'll be given a <u>business scenario</u>. You'll then need to carry out some kind of <u>task</u>.

2)   The task will probably be quite <u>open</u> (e.g. "design a web page for a local business"). There will always be <u>loads</u> of ways to approach the task.

Ten people could answer the same question in ten completely different ways, but all get full marks.

3)   But that doesn't mean you can just do what you like.
In some ways, the controlled assessment tasks will be quite <u>specific</u>.
For example, you might have to:
   - <u>Research and design</u> a new business website.
   - <u>Recommend</u> how a business could improve its communications.
   - <u>Research</u> the methods a business uses to communicate with its stakeholders, and decide which is the most important.

4)   So although you'll have a lot of <u>freedom</u> to decide for yourself how you want to <u>approach</u> the task, make sure you <u>remember</u> what it is you're <u>supposed</u> to be doing.

First You'll Do Research, Then You'll Produce a Document

Controlled assessment is an <u>exam</u>, but it could take a <u>few weeks</u> to finish. Weird.
There are <u>two parts</u> to the controlled assessment...

①   First you'll get <u>5-8 hours</u> to do some <u>research</u>.
   - You <u>can</u> ask your teacher for help during research time.
     (But your teacher <u>can't</u> help you with some things — like analysing your research.)
   - You <u>can</u> work in a group while you're <u>doing research</u>.
     <u>But</u>... make sure you get the information <u>you</u> need.

②   You'll then be given <u>3-4 hours</u> to produce your actual written-up (or typed-up) piece of <u>work</u>.
   - You'll be <u>supervised</u> by your teacher, but you <u>can't</u> ask for help with this.
   - And you <u>can't</u> work with friends. You're <u>not</u> even allowed to use other people's <u>research</u>.

Research task #1: learn what Controlled Assessment is about...

Controlled assessment tasks can look <u>daunting</u> — the key is to <u>keep your head</u> and <u>not panic</u>.
It also helps if you know what to <u>expect</u>. So it's definitely worth getting your head round all this stuff.

Written Exams

So... your brain is <u>stuffed</u> with wholesome Business and Communication Systems knowledge. Good. This page gives you a few tips on what to expect in the <u>written exam</u>, and how to <u>maximise your marks</u>.

There Are <u>Different Types</u> of Question to Look Out For

WRITTEN-ANSWER QUESTIONS

1) These are the types of question you'll spend <u>most of your time</u> answering.

2) For these questions, always look at the <u>marks available</u> and the <u>amount of space</u> you've been given. If a question's worth 10 marks, say, you'll have plenty of space for your answer — use it wisely.

3) Some short-answer questions will just ask you to remember and state a <u>fact</u>.

4) Other questions will give you a business <u>scenario</u> and ask you to <u>apply</u> your knowledge to that situation — but you <u>won't</u> be asked about anything you <u>haven't been taught</u>.

5) <u>Data-response</u> questions give you information (i.e. <u>data</u>) about a business — it might be a website, an advert, or even details about job applicants. You need to <u>apply</u> your knowledge to the data.

Make Sure You Understand These <u>Command Words</u>

All exam questions have a key "<u>command</u>" word that tells you what to do. For example...

These Test What You <u>Know</u>

Define or What is Meant By E.g. "What is meant by the term E-Commerce?" These questions are easy marks if you've learned all the <u>definitions</u>. You just have to know what the term <u>means</u>.

Describe These need a bit more than "Define..." questions — e.g. "Describe the main features of business administration." You'll have to make <u>several</u> points to answer this.

State or Identify These words ask for a <u>statement</u> — you don't need to back it up with evidence.

These Test What You <u>Understand</u>

Explain These questions involve giving <u>reasons</u>. You need to show you <u>understand</u> the link between things that happen in the world and the effects they have on businesses.

Analyse This means "Examine in detail." Make sure you talk about the <u>main features</u> of the thing you're analysing. Then explain <u>how</u> or <u>why</u> these features work together to lead to the end result.

These Test Your Ability to <u>Make Judgements</u>

Recommend   Discuss   Assess   Which is Most Likely/Appropriate   Evaluate

For these, you should always <u>back up</u> your points using your Business and Communications knowledge.

- Before you get started on your answer, make sure you've read the <u>whole question</u> carefully and you've <u>understood</u> what you're being asked to do. You'll lose marks if you take the wrong approach.

- In business situations, there are usually <u>advantages</u> and <u>disadvantages</u> to think about — to get all the marks, you'll need to give <u>both sides</u> of the argument before coming to a conclusion.

- <u>Link</u> your ideas together to build a <u>structured</u> argument.

All your questions about questions answered...

Questions, questions everywhere, and not much time to think. Different questions require <u>different types</u> of answers. My advice is to <u>read the question</u> and gather your thoughts <u>before</u> writing anything.

Computer-Based Assessment

You'll also have to do a computer-based assessment. It's a mixture of practical computer-based tasks and Business and Communication Systems theory. Makes a change from all that writing, though.

You'll Need to Complete Various Tasks on a Computer

1) Computer-based assessments are taken under test conditions — you have to work on your own.

2) But you'll be working on a computer — not writing on paper.

3) The exam paper will give you all the instructions you need to complete the various tasks.

4) You'll have to use some ready-made computer files — your teacher will tell you where these are stored.

5) You'll need to print your work for each question and hand it in at the end of the exam.

The Tasks are All Business-Related

The exam will test your practical software skills, and your understanding of the use of software in business.

1) Each of the tasks will be based on a business scenario.

2) You could be asked to produce a business document. Possible examples include:

- Text-based documents — e.g. a note, memo or business letter.
- Documents with text and graphics — e.g. a flyer, leaflet or advert.
- Slides for a business presentation.

You might be given text and pictures to use — or you might need to write or make them yourself.

3) You could be asked to carry out some kind of process. For example:

- Working with records in a database and producing a report.
- Doing calculations with numbers, and producing charts in a spreadsheet.
- Setting up a mail-merge for a set of business letters.

You'll probably be given some data to work with.

4) Some questions will ask you to explain and discuss software issues. For example:

- Explain why you've used particular formatting on a page.
- Discuss the pros and cons of software for a business (e.g. mail-merge, or presentation software).

In these questions, you're normally giving advice to a business — you might need to do this in a letter or a memo.

Don't Lose Easy Marks

In the exam, don't forget to do the easy things well.

1) **READ THE INSTRUCTIONS CAREFULLY** — both the general instructions at the start of the paper, and the instructions for each task. There are some easy marks on these papers — don't throw them away.

2) **DO EXACTLY AS YOU'RE TOLD** — some questions will ask you to use a particular format (e.g. landscape). Or you might need to save your work using a particular filename. Follow the instructions to the letter. And make sure you include your name and candidate number when told.

3) **TAKE CARE WHEN SAVING** — don't save over the top of files you might need to use again or hand in.

4) **CHECK YOUR PRINTOUTS** — it's surprisingly easy to miss mistakes on screen — so check your printouts carefully before you hand them in.

Time to face some hard questions about software...

Computer-based assessments test how well you know your way around software, so make sure you know how to use all the tools and features in Sections 7 to 10. But you might also have to explain how software can be useful in business — so make sure you revise that side of things too. Okay, that's all I have to say.

Index

Index